RAND

T0096849

Taking Charge

*A Bipartisan Report
to the President–Elect
on Foreign Policy and
National Security*

Transition 2001

Frank Carlucci, Robert Hunter,
Zalmay Khalilzad, co-chairs

The ideas and recommendations included in this report are the work of more than 50 American leaders in foreign policy and national security. This is a diverse group of individuals, drawn from across the political spectrum, who have served the nation in public service or who come from the worlds of academia and policy analysis—all with knowledge, experience, and engagement in critical U.S. foreign policy and national security debates. They were invited by RAND to identify the most important challenges for the new U.S. president, to suggest priorities, to propose and discuss the range of alternative choices, and, where there is collective agreement, to recommend specific courses of action. The deliberations of the group were informed by some twenty-five papers commissioned by the panel and largely based on RAND research. This publication was supported by RAND using its own funds.

ISBN: 0-8330-2956-8

Cover design by Eric Handel/LMNOP

Published 2001 by RAND
1700 Main Street, P.O. Box 2138, Santa Monica, CA 90407-2138
1200 South Hayes Street, Arlington, VA 22202-5050
RAND URL: http://www.rand.org/
To order RAND documents or to obtain additional information,
contact Distribution Services: Telephone: (310) 451-7002;
Fax: (310) 451-6915; Internet: order@rand.org

Transition 2001 is a bipartisan panel of about 60 American leaders in the areas of foreign and defense policy, co-chaired by Frank Carlucci, Robert Hunter, and Zalmay Khalilzad and coordinated by Jeremy Shapiro. The convening of the panel stemmed from the belief that this presidential transition comes at a critical time for America's role in the world—a time, also, when there is special value in trying to forge as much bipartisan agreement as possible on the central tenets of U.S. foreign and national security policy. Accordingly, our purpose was to survey the principal challenges that the United States will face abroad in the years immediately ahead and to recommend specific actions that the new president could take in the early days of his administration. Such decisive early action will be critical for setting U.S. foreign and national security policy on the right path for the balance of his term and beyond.

To conduct its work, the panel commissioned more than 25 discussion papers on key issues and areas, prepared by RAND staff and others, to provide analyses of the most critical foreign and national security issues facing the United States, both during the first part of the new administration and in the long term. The panel met four times from February to October 2000 to discuss the most critical issues. The result of the panel's work is this report and an accompanying volume of the discussion papers. The report outlines what we have determined to be the most important national security challenges for the new administration, suggests priorities, and, where we could reach consensus, recommends specific courses of action. It is our hope that this report can make a signal contribution by helping to focus attention on key priorities and, in the process, helping to create bipartisan support for American foreign and defense policy.

THE TRANSITION 2001 PANEL

The following members of the panel have endorsed the basic content of the report:

Gordon M. Adams, George Washington University

Kenneth L. Adelman, former Director, ACDA

J. Brian Atwood, Citizens International

Norman R. Augustine, retired Chairman and CEO of Lockheed Martin Corporation

Jeremy R. Azrael, RAND

Elizabeth Frawley Bagley, former U.S. Ambassador to Portugal and Department of State Senior Advisor

Robert Bates, former corporate secretary, Mobil Corporation

Barry M. Blechman, DFI International

Harold Brown, CSIS

Richard Burt, IEP Advisors, LLP

Daniel L. Byman, RAND

Frank C. Carlucci, The Carlyle Group

Ashton Carter, Harvard University

David S.C. Chu, RAND

Natalie W. Crawford, RAND

Lynn E. Davis, RAND

Thomas A. Dine, Radio Free Europe/Radio Liberty

Marc Ginsberg, APCO Global Ventures

David C. Gompert, RAND Europe

Jerrold D. Green, RAND

William Harrop, former U.S. Ambassador

Robert E. Hunter, RAND

Jeffrey A. Isaacson, RAND

Bruce W. Jentleson, Duke University

Zalmay M. Khalilzad, RAND

F. Stephen Larrabee, RAND

Mel Levine, Gibson, Dunn, & Crutcher LLP

Samuel W. Lewis, American Academy of Diplomacy

Jessica Tuchman Mathews, Carnegie Endowment for International Peace *(with dissent)*

Dave McCurdy, Electronic Industries Alliance

David A. Ochmanek, RAND

Diann H. Painter, former chief economist, Mobil Corporation

Angel Rabasa, RAND

Michael D. Rich, RAND

John E. Rielly, Chicago Council on Foreign Relations

Robert Satloff, Washington Institute for Near East Policy

Jeremy Shapiro, RAND

David Skaggs, The Aspen Institute *(with dissent)*

Marin J. Strmecki, Smith Richardson Foundation

Loren B. Thompson, Lexington Institute

James A. Thomson, RAND

Ted Van Dyk, Claremont Graduate University and UCLA

Edward L. Warner, RAND

Harlan K. Ullman, CNA and CSIS *(with comment)*

Please note that endorsement of the report by these individuals does not constitute an endorsement by their affiliated organizations.

The following members of the panel participated in the process, but due to their affiliation could not endorse the report:

Thomas E. Donilon, Fannie Mae

Albert Eisele, *The Hill*

Richard N. Haass, The Brookings Institution

Rita E. Hauser, The Hauser Foundation

Harriet Hentges, U.S. Institute of Peace

Anthony Lake, Georgetown University

Richard H. Solomon, U.S. Institute of Peace

Paul A. Volcker, former Chairman of the Board of Governors of the Federal Reserve System

Paul D. Wolfowitz, John Hopkins School of Advanced International Studies

Dov S. Zakheim, System Planning Corporation

CONTENTS

TRANSMITTAL LETTER TO THE PRESIDENT-ELECT

Dear Mr. President-elect:

This report has been prepared by a bipartisan group of Americans with extensive foreign policy experience in and out of government. It is designed to assist you as you prepare to take charge of U.S. foreign and national security policy. We have made proposals on both process and policy in a few key areas where we believe your early action will be important in determining the nation's ability to protect and promote its interests for the balance of your presidency and beyond. These proposals are detailed in the accompanying report. This letter summarizes our recommendations.

Setting a Direction. You come to office at a time of double challenge: both to deal effectively with classical problems of power and purpose and to seize the opportunities provided by profound changes—from advances in information technology to "globalization." We recommend that, early in your administration, you set an overall direction for U.S. foreign policy and national security and begin building bipartisan support for it. We advocate selective global leadership by the United States, coupled with strengthened and revitalized alliances. America should seek to preclude the rise of a hostile global rival or a hostile global alliance. At the same time, America should help focus its democratic alliances on new threats, challenges, and opportunities, while preparing its allies for increasingly shared responsibility and leadership. Without our democratic allies, many emerging global issues would likely prove to be beyond our ability to manage. But together with them, the United States will gain unparalleled ability to respond to tomorrow's demands and to shape the future. We believe that, together with our allies, your administration should focus on integrating Russia and China into the current international system and strengthening relations with India; encouraging the transformation of the major states that are in flux into responsible members of the international community; constraining regional troublemakers; continuing to play the role of peacemaker; adapting to the new global economy and meeting the full agenda of issues presented by globalization; promoting democracy and fundamental human values; seeking the reduction of weapons of mass destruction (WMD) and missiles—especially in the hands of hostile states; and protecting the United States, its forces, and its allies against WMD and missile attack.

Personnel and Organization. We recommend that, most immediately, you create your core team and determine the way that you want its members to work together—and for you. We suggest that you select your key foreign policy and national security officials as a team and announce them together by early December. To recruit top-flight people for senior office, we advise that you not impose any more impediments to service, including conflict-of-interest regulations, and that you review—with an eye to reform—those requirements that fall within your discretion. You should also ensure that the clearance process for senior officials moves rapidly within the White House and the cabinet departments—where more delays take place than in the Senate.

We believe that the current National Security Council (NSC) system is highly flexible and gives you wide latitude—including the latitude to add officials from "nontraditional" areas. We thus counsel against making major changes at the outset of your administration. We believe, however, that the NSC should not take on an operational role and that you should consider creating a new office in the NSC: a Strategic Planning Office. Finally, we recommend that you immediately order a thorough review of all key aspects of U.S. foreign and national security policy.

We also recommend that you submit to Congress an integrated "foreign policy and national security budget"—even if at first in broad outline—with explanations of connections, choices, and tradeoffs among different instruments of foreign policy and national security. We recommend that, on the basis of this submission, you ask Congress for a critically needed 20 percent increase in nonmilitary spending on foreign policy and national security (the so-called "150 account").

Critical Decisions. Much of the world will give you a grace period at the outset of your administration. But we believe that in a few areas, you will need to prepare rapidly for reaching decisions with long-range implications. We judge three to be most critical:

- **Missile Defenses.** Because of the intensity of debate about National Missile Defense (NMD), it is important to seize control of this issue immediately. Indeed, mishandling this issue could have severe consequences across a wide range of concerns, including the nation's military security and relations with the allies, Russia, and China. Opinions within our panel vary about the best alternatives for NMD. We do concur that the issue merits a fresh look and that, promptly after inauguration, you should mandate a comprehensive review of all critical factors. At the same time, we recommend that you proceed with theater missile defense, to protect deployed U.S. forces, allies, and friends.

- **Taking Charge at Defense.** The timetable of defense budgeting means that critical decisions affecting much of your time in office are being made even before your inauguration. We recommend that to take charge, you take three steps in parallel. First, develop immediately an overall, if rudimentary, strategic game plan for U.S. foreign and national security policy. Second, use this game plan to guide you through revision of the Fiscal Year 2002 defense budget, which the Pentagon has nearly completed, for April submission to Congress. Finally, provide firm direction for the basic long-range defense planning document—the Quadrennial Defense Review (QDR)—due to Congress in September, and encourage the Secretary of Defense to explore options that challenge established modes of thought in conducting that review.

- **Arab-Israeli Peacemaking.** If fighting continues in the Middle East, the first task must be to help stop it. When peacemaking becomes possible, all parties will look to the United States for leadership and diplomatic engagement. We recommend that you start with a thorough internal review of the alternatives, get your negotiating team in place, and make clear some central principles—e.g., U.S. commitment to Israel's security, to building peace, to supporting the prosperity of all in the region, and to seeing the violence stop before the peace process can resume. The parties will expect you to play a direct role at some point, but you should reserve judgment about when this could be most effective.

Possible Crises. In addition to the Arab-Israeli conflict, you may face other immediate crises or opportunities. We single out four: Saddam Hussein may try some form of military action or reductions in Iraqi oil exports. Incidents in the Taiwan Strait could generate a crisis between Taiwan and China. You could face either a crisis in Korea or, as appears more likely, an opportunity for major improvement. You could also confront a crisis in Colombia, with wider regional implications, stemming from the central government's loss of control over large parts of the country.

On Iraq, we recommend that you be prepared to use the Strategic Petroleum Reserve and seek an understanding with Saudi Arabia and others to expand oil production; and that, if provoked by Saddam Hussein, the United States attack a wider range of strategic and military targets to demonstrate resolve and deter further challenges. On Taiwan, we recommend stating clearly to both parties where the United States stands: that the United States opposes unilateral moves toward independence by Taiwan but will support Taiwan in the event of an unprovoked Chinese attack. On Korea, the potential end-game of the conflict is an intra-Korean issue to be solved by the two countries, but we believe that the United States should communicate its interests—e.g., to gain an end to WMD and ballistic missile programs in the North, and an agreement with Seoul about the size and character of the U.S. force posture after a diplomatic breakthrough. On Colombia, we recommend that the United States expand its support for Plan Colombia and develop a web of cooperation with concerned Latin American states but commit no U.S. combat forces.

Sustaining a Preeminent Military. Our military forces face many looming challenges and need to be strengthened. Many of the military's premier platforms are becoming obsolete. Operating costs of current forces are high and growing, and deployments for peacekeeping and humanitarian intervention have imposed significant burdens, while threats have grown more diverse. With the proliferation of longer-range missiles and more lethal weapons, expeditionary operations are becoming more challenging.

We believe that the strengthening of U.S. forces should take place in the context of a transformation of American security strategy and defense posture—taking them firmly beyond the Cold War. U.S. forces must be able to deploy quickly to various theaters and win against a wide range of potential adversaries. We judge that, unless you fundamentally change the current strategy or attempt a new approach to military operations that places greater emphasis on new technologies, a sizable modernization bill cannot be avoided. In each of the next several years, the Defense Department will need about $30 billion more for procurement and $5–10 billion more for real property maintenance, recruitment, pay and retirement, and medical care—about a 10 percent increase in real terms.

We also believe that U.S. force planning should take greater account of the potential capabilities of U.S. allies to achieve greater interoperability and to relieve some burdens. We also support far-reaching changes in the transatlantic regime for defense exports and investments, including more flexibility in U.S. transfers of high technology.

To deal with recruitment and retention problems, we recommend targeted pay raises, especially those aimed at skilled enlisted personnel. To preserve our defense industrial base, we suggest that you direct the Defense Department to reduce as much as possible the administrative burdens of doing business with it and make defense research and development contracts profitable in their own right. You also have a major opportunity to rationalize defense by restarting the Base Realignment and Closure (BRAC) process, seeking congressional authority early in your administration, on the basis of an independent commission, to develop a non-amendable package.

A Broader U.S.-European Strategic Partnership. After the United States, Western Europe is the repository of the world's greatest concentration of economic capacity, military strength, and ability to undertake efforts in other regions. Thus, we recommend that early in your administration, you begin a strategic dialogue directly with the European Union (EU), in addition to the central U.S. strategic engagement with the NATO allies. This can create the basis for common approaches and joint action, both regionally and functionally—e.g., for helping to deal with sub-Saharan Africa's daunting challenges. An opportune time to launch this initiative is at the projected U.S.-EU summit in Stockholm in June.

The next NATO summit is projected for 2002; at this summit, the allies will review progress toward membership made by the current nine applicants. To be successful, however, as leader of the alliance, the United States would need to lay the groundwork in 2001 for a comprehensive approach to European security. This includes building on the Partnership for Peace; the NATO-Ukraine Charter; the U.S.-Baltic Charter; and the NATO-Russia relationship—while preserving NATO's right to decide which countries to admit to membership. We recommend that you support the development of the European Security and Defense Policy (ESDP) but also press the Europeans to accelerate their force modernization and increase their capabilities for power projection.

The Balkans remain the most troubled part of Europe, and transition in Belgrade has not ended the challenge to regional security. We counsel against assuming that the stabilization forces in Bosnia and Kosovo can soon depart. The Transition 2001 panel divides, however, on the appropriate U.S. role in the Balkans; some argue that the United States should continue its force deployments, within an agreed common NATO policy; others argue that the United States should progressively turn over to the European allies responsibility for providing ground forces for the Balkans. Most difficult is the future of Kosovo—whether it remains a part of Serbia or becomes independent. Your administration will be expected to take the lead; you should decide early whether the United States favors independence, autonomy, or some third alternative.

Recasting U.S. Alliances in Asia. We recommend that, soon after inauguration, you direct a basic review of U.S. strategy throughout Asia. Of most immediate concern, if there are rapid changes in Korea, U.S. forces based there and in Japan will be under increasing political pressure. The United States will continue to need forward bases in Asia to help provide stability and prevent hegemony by any regional power. We suggest a five-part strategy: The United States should reaffirm its existing Asian bilateral alliances. It should support Japan's efforts to revise its constitution, to allow it to expand its security horizon beyond territorial defense and to acquire appropriate capabilities for supporting coalition operations. The United States should enhance ties among its bilateral alliance partners and important relations in the region. The United States should identify in advance and prepare to implement a strategy for dealing with any situations that might tempt others to use force—e.g., the Taiwan Straits or territorial disputes, as in the South China Sea. And the United States should promote an inclusive security dialogue among as broad a range as possible of Asian states. Finally, implementing this strategy in Asia will require some revisions to the regional U.S. military posture. The focus will have to be shifted broadly southward, while alliances with Japan and South Korea are recast and new access arrangements are created elsewhere in Asia.

Powers in Flux. Your administration should also begin formulating long-term policies toward several major countries that are of great strategic interest to the United States and whose domestic or international positions are in flux. We single out several as most critical for efforts in 2001:

- **Russia.** We believe that basic U.S. policy should be to anchor Russia in the West and, if it will respond, to build a positive political and military relationship with it. We suggest that, together with allies, the United States should seek reductions in the Russian nuclear arsenal, firm control over that arsenal, reforms within the Russian military, and an end to any Russian role in the proliferation of nuclear weapons or other WMD. Economic assistance from the United States and its allies can, with careful monitoring, be useful and productive and serve Western interests; and we recommend that you search for areas of global cooperation with Russia. The United States also needs to secure Western interests in the Transcaucasus and Central Asia—promoting the independence of these eight countries but counseling them on creating stable relations with Russia.

- **China.** We recommend that, in cooperation with regional allies, the United States should pursue a mixed strategy toward China that is neither pure engagement nor pure containment. This would include engaging China through commerce and encouragement of increased economic and political development; developing a strategic dialogue with China across the full range of issues and strengthening military-to-military ties; exploring with China, both bilaterally and with other nations, joint projects that can advance common interests; putting heavy emphasis on the development of democracy in China, including political and media freedoms and respect for human rights; hedging against a Chinese push for regional domination; and discouraging Chinese assistance in the spread of missile technology. If China chooses to cooperate within the current international system and becomes democratic, this mixed strategy could evolve into mutual accommodation and partnership. If China becomes a hostile power bent on regional domination, the U.S. posture could evolve into containment.

- **India and Pakistan.** We recommend that your South Asia policy begin by decoupling India and Pakistan in U.S. calculations. U.S. relations with each state should be governed by an assessment of the intrinsic value of each country to American interests. India is becoming a major Asian power and therefore warrants an increased level of engagement and appreciation of its potential for both collaboration and resistance across a much larger canvas than South Asia. By contrast, Pakistan is in serious crisis and is pursuing policies counter to important U.S. interests. The United States should increase pressure on Islamabad to stop support for the Taliban, to cooperate in the fight against terrorism, to show restraint in Kashmir, and to focus on solving its own internal problems.

- **Iraq and Iran.** Changing circumstances in the Persian Gulf—including erosion of the sanctions regime against Iraq and domestic political change in Iran—call for a reappraisal of the U.S. dual-containment policy, maintaining the premise that a critical long-term goal is to maintain regional stability and prevent the domination of the Persian Gulf by a hostile power. We recommend that the reappraisal assess whether regime change in Iraq is necessary to U.S. long-term goals and, if so, how to bring it about and the potential costs. The review should also consider whether U.S. goals can be achieved by strict containment of Iraq and what the risks would be, as well as what role U.S. allies, especially in Europe, might play in containing Iraq. Containment of Iraq could be aided by an Iran that is prepared to rejoin the international community and end support for terrorism, opposi-

tion to the Arab-Israeli peace process, and development of nuclear weapons and long-range missiles. The United States also
shares an interest with Iran in helping to stabilize Afghanistan.
Your administration should be prepared either to contain Iran or
to seize the opportunity if Iran becomes interested in rapprochement. The latter means being ready with specific ideas,
such as increasing U.S. investments in Iranian infrastructure,
ending U.S. opposition to building an energy pipeline through
Iran from Central Asia, achieving cooperation between the
United States and Iran on containing Iraq, and cooperating on
measures to stabilize Afghanistan.

- **Indonesia.** Indonesia is undergoing a political transformation
  that could change the geostrategic shape of Asia. Severe instability in, or a breakup of, Indonesia could disrupt trade and investment flows throughout Asia, generate widespread violence, create massive refugee flows, encourage secessionist movements
  throughout Southeast Asia, and damage the progress of democracy in the region. Therefore, we believe that helping to avoid
  political collapse in Indonesia and keeping democratic reforms
  on track should be a high U.S. priority. We recommend four
  elements: keeping patience with the limited ability of the Indonesian government to move quickly toward democracy; supporting Indonesia's economic recovery and territorial integrity;
  engaging the Indonesian military; and helping to restore a constructive Indonesian role in regional security.

The New Global Agenda. The end of the Cold War and recent
changes in the global economy have expanded the international
agenda. Globalization will have a growing impact on definitions of
U.S. "foreign policy," the instruments available, the relative degree of
control over events exercised by governments as opposed to the
private sector and nongovernmental organizations (NGOs), and
interconnections between events in different parts of the world. We
believe that the U.S. response—and U.S. leadership—should have
several elements:

- **Fostering Global Economic Order.** We recommend that early in
  your administration, you seek "fast-track" trade negotiating authority from Congress, secure support from key allies on management of multilateral negotiations, engage U.S. groups with

critical interests, and work to ensure that less influential countries and NGOs gain appropriate access to the negotiations. We also recommend that you promote reforms in the international financial institutions to ensure that they are accountable to their constituencies in both lending and borrowing countries; that their funds are stimulating balanced and sustainable growth; and that these funds are being neither diverted or stolen by host-country officials nor allocated to inefficient or socially irresponsible uses. Finally, we recommend that you take proactive measures to extend and deepen economic ties with Latin America, and especially with Mexico, for the purposes of fostering a stable, democratic, and free-market-oriented hemisphere. The key components of this policy would include efforts to promote balanced and sustainable economic development, to ensure monetary stability, to extend and deepen free trade areas throughout Latin America, and to promote a hemispheric security community.

- **Nontraditional Threats and Opportunities.** A number of new developments may pose severe challenges to Western society, including uncontrolled migration across borders and regions, international crime, disease—especially pandemics like AIDS and malaria, and issues of the environment. Many of these problems will particularly afflict Africa, and thus that continent is important, despite the limited U.S. security interests there. So far, there is no consensus that these challenges pose national security threats. Under any circumstances, however, your leadership will be critical in raising awareness of these challenges, both at home and abroad. Meanwhile, the potential to spread democracy and human rights represents the major opportunity of the age to create a better world. We believe that the United States should remain the foremost champion of democratic development, providing vigorous support for global democracy-based institutions and follow-up to the June 2000 World Democracy Conference.

- **Asymmetric Warfare.** During your administration, key challenges to the security of the United States, its allies, and its friends can come from so-called asymmetrical warfare, conducted by a variety of countries and non-state actors, in part as a response to U.S. military dominance. Three areas are most important: terrorism, including terrorism within the United States; cyber threats to critical infrastructure; and WMD and the means of delivering them. We believe that successful responses to these problems will require U.S. leadership in promoting greater cooperation among the major industrial countries. We also recommend that you mandate cooperation among domestic law enforcement, intelligence, economic, and diplomatic assets to combat both terrorism and WMD and missile proliferation. Internationally, we suggest that the U.S. work to strengthen the Biological Weapons Convention, press Russia to stop providing assistance to Iran for its nuclear program, and discourage Chinese and Russian assistance in the spread of missile technology.

- **Developing International Institutions.** Finally, the United States faces a continuing challenge to remain as free as possible of external threats and to be influential in shaping the global environment to positive ends. We believe that one long-term means is particularly critical: U.S. leadership in building international institutions, practices, attitudes, and processes—NATO is one model—that will benefit the United States because they also benefit other countries. Reinvigorating the process of institutional development will require paying the dues that the United States owes to the United Nations, while pressing for needed institutional reforms.

Chapter One

INTRODUCTION: SETTING DIRECTIONS FOR THE GLOBAL ERA

You are taking office at a unique and critical time for the United States and its engagement abroad. Your leadership and America's role during the next few years can be decisive in shaping the world for the next generation and beyond. If you can be ready by January 20 to deploy the full powers of the presidency to start exercising this leadership, you will be better placed to meet the immense opportunities that our nation now faces. This report is intended to assist you in that effort.

Ten years after the end of the Cold War, the United States finds itself with military, economic, political, and even cultural power that is unrivaled. But we are still struggling to understand what we must do abroad in support of our interests and values, how we can help shape the kind of world in which we want to live, and what the limits of our power are. In the past decade, we learned anew that America cannot retreat from the world, that isolationism is impossible. We learned that American economic and military strength is as important as ever and that much of the world still depends on us to be engaged—and to lead.

Challenges to U.S. national security and that of allies and friends have, in some cases, changed in character, but they have not disappeared. Conflict has continued, even intensified, in many parts of the world that are significant to the United States. While the Soviet Union is gone, Russia has not been anchored in the West and will still be a critical factor in determining whether we can expect a peaceful future. Other countries, notably China and India, are seeking to enhance their status as great powers. Several important regional powers—in particular, Pakistan, Iran, and Indonesia—are in a state of flux. What happens *within* these countries will be critical, if not decisive, in determining what they do abroad.

Moreover, hostile states are challenging international norms in several regions. The potential spread of weapons of mass destruction (WMD), new types of weapons, and the means of employing them, and the persistence and ingenuity of international terrorism have created the phenomenon of asymmetrical warfare. In sum, classic problems of power and security will continue to have an impact on America's interests and those of its friends and allies.

At the same time, as you assume the presidency, one of history's more profound revolutions, unleashed largely by swift and radical advances in technology, is causing changes, both within societies and in the world as a whole, that may prove as profound as those that followed the Industrial Revolution two centuries ago, but whose precise character and impact can now be only partly understood. Globalization is transforming the nature of international life in finance and economics, and increasingly in politics and security; disparities of wealth are growing within many societies and, in some cases, between advanced and developing states. Certain social, political, and religious forces are having a growing impact. Governments are less in control of foreign policy than they were only a few years ago; global politics is increasingly being shaped by nongovernmental organizations (NGOs) and by private-sector and financial entities that transcend traditional state borders. For most countries, sovereignty is eroding—in some places, such as the European Union (EU), by design; elsewhere, as an unintended consequence of the digital age. Resentment of globalization is on the rise and has produced increased anti-Americanism, since the United States is perceived as its architect. Should this trend grow, it could hamper efforts at building new global trading and financial institutions that are necessary to expand and spread prosperity around the world.

Newer concerns, including cross-border crime and illegal narcotics trafficking, threats in cyberspace, the challenge of mass migration, the rise of religious extremism, humanitarian disasters, failed states and warlordism, environmental degradation, and the spread of disease, are all part of the new international security agenda. There is no national consensus on how the United States should balance the pursuit of its own traditional interests and these newer international concerns.

In short, we live in a complex and demanding age, full of both opportunity and peril. Indeed, we may not now foresee many of the challenges that will emerge in the next several years. Meanwhile, American power and position, while today unrivaled, will not automatically be sustained, but will be deeply affected both by what the United States does and by how others respond. Above all, in the years just ahead, we must learn how to translate our great power into lasting influence.

Yet despite the responsibilities of leadership that necessarily now fall on U.S. shoulders, American power and will cannot on their own suffice to meet and master the array of global demands that challenge U.S. interests, those of our friends and allies, and the welfare of the planet as a whole. We, the members of the Transition 2001 panel, thus advocate a method as much as a vision: selective global leadership by the United States, coupled with strengthened and revitalized alliances. America should seek to preclude the rise of a hostile global rival or a hostile global alliance while at the same time transforming its democratic alliances by focusing them on new threats, challenges, and opportunities and preparing them for increasingly joint or shared leadership. Together with its democratic allies, the United States will have unparalleled ability to respond to tomorrow's demands. Without those allies, many emerging global issues will prove to be beyond our ability to manage. Therefore, maintaining, strengthening, and extending these alliances is essential to America's future and should be the bedrock of U.S. engagement abroad. We believe that, together with our allies, your administration should focus on integrating Russia and China into the current international system and strengthening relations with India; encouraging the transformation of the major states that are in flux into responsible members of the international community; constraining regional troublemakers; continuing to play the role of peacemaker; adapting to the new global economy and meeting the full agenda of issues presented by globalization; promoting democracy and fundamental human values; seeking the reduction of WMD and missiles—especially in the hands of hostile states; and protecting the United States, our forces, and our allies against WMD and missile attack.

As president of the United States, you will have the responsibility for dealing, at one and the same time, with both the old and the new—the classic world of relations among states and power politics, and the newer world of globalization and of other emerging forces in international society. Like your predecessors, you will lead the nation in determining—and integrating—America's interests and values in the outside world, setting priorities, understanding interrelationships and tradeoffs, making choices, and building political support—both within Congress and among the American people—for those choices.

This report is designed to help guide you through the period when you are taking charge of your new administration in foreign and national security policy and are beginning to put that policy on a firm course to achieve the goals you set for the nation. We have placed heavy emphasis on process: what you need to do to be able to govern at home and to lead abroad. But we also propose key requirements of policy, especially those we judge to be most important for the United States in the next several years, since the policy choices you make in your first few months in office may well determine your ability to be successful during the balance of your presidency.

This report is organized as follows:

- Immediate steps to organize and staff your administration in foreign policy and national security and to begin building a productive relationship with Congress.

- Possible themes for your first presentations to the nation and the world before inauguration, as an early act of leadership.

- Decisions you will need to make—or prepare to make—at the beginning of your administration.

- Possible international crises and opportunities you could face very soon, and suggestions for dealing with them.

- Steps to take early in your administration in order to pursue long-term goals in critical areas.

We do not propose here a full and comprehensive set of foreign and national security policies—this is not an exhaustive "laundry list" of ideas. Instead, we have focused on what we believe are the most important areas and actions for your engagement and decision either before your inauguration or in the first few months of your presidency. We believe that these are the most important priorities for your leadership of the nation.

Chapter Two

FIRST STEPS: THE TRANSITION AND AFTER INAUGURATION

PEOPLE AND PROCESS

The most immediate task in foreign policy and national security is to create the core team and to determine the way that you want them to work together—and for you. These key officials and the working relationships among them must be firmly in place before you can exercise leadership in foreign affairs or carry out your duties as commander-in-chief. This task should be completed before the inauguration.

We suggest that you select your top foreign policy and national security officials as a team and announce them together: the Secretaries of State and Defense, your National Security Advisor, and—with the increased importance of economic issues for America's role abroad—the Secretary of the Treasury and the Director of the National Economic Council (NEC). You may also wish to add your Director of Central Intelligence and your Ambassador to the United Nations, as well as your chief of staff, domestic policy director, and assistant for congressional relations. These choices will send powerful messages to foreign capitals, to financial markets, and to the American people.

Making these choices promptly is important for an additional reason: Unless you decide to retain some top officials from the current administration, the only two senior members of the foreign policy team who can start work immediately on Inauguration Day are the members of the White House staff, namely the National Security Advisor and the Director of the NEC. The others require Senate confirmation. To ensure speedy confirmation of cabinet-level and other senior appointees, you should consider consulting early with leaders in the Senate, and also in the House. This will also give you the chance to start rebuilding what has been a frayed relationship between the White House and Congress.

No less important is the organization of decisionmaking in foreign policy and national security. Since 1947, this has been done through the National Security Council (NSC) and a series of committees, the most important of which are now called the Principals' Committee and a Deputies' Committee, the former chaired by the NSC Advisor, the latter by his or her deputy. In the aftermath of the Cold War, and facing the vast array of challenges that do not fit within a traditional definition of "national security," the United States needs a system of management and decisionmaking that can encompass both the old and the new demands of policy. At the outset—and until you determine whether you are being well served—you can achieve this goal by adding officials to the structure of the NSC, including people from "nontraditional" areas, who represent the full range of your agenda. In fact, the current NSC system is highly flexible and gives you wide latitude; it can enable you to make choices, integrate policy, and exercise leadership across a broad range of issues. *Thus, we counsel against trying to change the basic NSC system at the outset of your administration.* Experience will best inform you whether that is needed. You should consider setting out your decisions concerning the NSC in a Presidential Decision Directive or, for greater effect, an Executive Order.

We do recommend that you create a new body, within the NSC, charged with strategic analysis, long-range planning, and assessment of tradeoffs among the multiple issues that make up "national security" in the post–Cold War world. Classically, the lack of any such institutional capacity in the White House has been a cardinal weakness of presidential leadership in foreign affairs: The short term tends to drive out the long term. We believe that a capacity for strategic analysis and long-range planning will be created only if you insist upon it, appoint able staff under the chairmanship of the National Security Advisor, ensure that they fit within the decisionmaking process, and demonstrate that their work is important to you. This new body—a Strategic Planning

Office—can provide you and the members of the NSC with a broad, long-term perspective; it should also draw upon the work of the National Intelligence Council (NIC), as well as policy planning staffs in the cabinet departments engaged abroad, and thus improve interagency coordination on longer-term issues.

Immediately on taking office, you should also consider directing a fundamental review of all major aspects of America's engagement in the world. Other presidents have begun with an effort to rethink basic policies, although none has done so thoroughly for decades. In view of the major changes in the world since the end of the Cold War, including the onset of globalization, this is a critical moment to conduct such a review, begin developing long-range strategies for U.S. engagement abroad, and—in the process—involve both the Congress and the American people.

Finally, because of changes in global society and the nature of American involvement and presence, U.S. foreign policy will now be importantly affected by decisions made and carried out by nongovernmental organizations (NGOs) and the private sector, often without a direct role by the U.S. government. This is already true in international finance, global business, and areas such as human rights, economic development, and democratization; globalization will accelerate the process and carry it to a wide and expanding range of activities. You should create a new body within the Executive Office of the President, analogous to the Office of Science and Technology Policy, to foster policy consideration of NGO and private sector activities, to help inform policy choices, and to provide for liaison with these groups.

Staffing the Administration in Foreign Policy and National Security

Among the most consequential choices you will ever make in foreign policy and national security will be the people you pick as your senior officials. They can set a tone—and establish a good deal of the substance—for your entire term of office. To ensure your capacity to lead, we suggest that you build the key elements of this team as rapidly as possible, choosing your cabinet-level officials no later than early December. We also recommend that you immediately select a head of the White House Office of Presidential Personnel who has senior-level experience in managing a complex personnel-recruiting process.

In the post–Cold War world, your effectiveness will depend in part on choosing at least one cabinet-level official—either the National Security Advisor or the Secretary of State—with capacity and experience in high-level strategic analysis and integration of policy. Even if you choose to provide regular, hands-on strategic direction of policy, you will be aided greatly by having such a top official. You should consider making clear, however, that neither the National Security Advisor nor the NSC staff will have operational responsibilities; that role should be clearly reserved to the cabinet departments, and you should vest primacy in the conduct of foreign affairs in the Secretary of State. By the same token, in recent years, representatives from a wide range of government agencies have proliferated at U.S. embassies and other missions abroad; we suggest that you affirm the authority of U.S. ambassadors as your principal representatives abroad, charged with overseeing and coordinating the overall conduct of U.S. diplomacy at their missions.

You will also benefit from deciding whether you want a core team that will tend to produce consensus on broad policy matters (thus reducing the attention you will need to pay on a routine basis), or a team that will sharpen debate and press a wide range of issues to you for resolution (thus ensuring that you will have to be regularly engaged). We judge that, in the new age, you, as president, will need to be deeply engaged, on a sustained basis, in the making and carrying out of foreign policy.

As with the staffing of other departments and agencies, a key issue is how deeply to involve yourself and your White House staff in the selection of officials immediately subordinate to the cabinet-level national security officials. Some presidents have entrusted their cabinet secretaries with choosing their own teams, with the White House playing only an overseeing role. Others have retained significant authority for themselves, sharing in the choice of key sub-cabinet officials, in order to demonstrate that these officials clearly owe their appointments, and their loyalty, to the president and not just to a cabinet secretary.

Even more than in other areas, a high premium should be placed on expertise and experience in key appointments in foreign policy and national security.   Political talents, especially for dealing with Congress and explaining policy publicly, are valuable assets in the Secretaries of State and Defense. But in the overall staffing of the key departments and agencies, great emphasis should be placed on knowledge, background, and experience. Many critical decisions do not primarily reflect political choices, a role for constituencies, or key factors that are essentially limited to the confines of the United States and its domestic politics—as is usually the case in domestic policy—but depend, rather, on a capacity both to respond effectively to events and actions emanating from abroad and to craft coherent strategies for the United States in the world. You will also need talented people from nontraditional areas, to ensure that issues such as globalization, as well as the congeries of newer concerns, can be dealt with effectively within the overall framework of U.S. foreign policy.

For many years, between one-quarter and one-third of ambassadorial appointees have come from the ranks of political supporters. However, we suggest that, in appointing ambassadors, you be sensitive to relations with particular countries where the ambassadors' knowledge and expertise are important for the successful pursuit of U.S. goals, as well as to those countries where the U.S. ambassador's personal or political relationship with the president is highly prized. You should consider creating an independent advisory panel to vet possible ambassadorial appointees, both career and political; this can help search out talent and provide you with some insulation from the politics of appointment.

In recent years, the requirements of qualifying for senior-level government appointment, whether imposed by law or by presidential decision, have become increasingly complex, cumbersome, and often self-defeating, in that they have dramatically reduced the ranks of talented Americans who are prepared to accept public service. Conflict-of-interest regulations have become especially burdensome and inhibiting. As president-elect, you cannot escape most of the complex requirements for government service that have built up over time; *but we strongly believe that you should resist imposing any more requirements and, as soon as possible, you should review—with an eye to reform—those that fall within your discretion.* We also recommend that you ensure that the clearance process for senior officials moves rapidly within the White House and the cabinet departments, and that nominations reach the Senate as soon as possible. Indeed, most delays in qualifying senior officials occur in the Executive branch, not in the Senate. Later, you should consider seeking congressional support in reducing the burdens on government service, including excessive conflict-of-interest regulations, and in increasing the financial compensation.

Forging Effective Relations with Congress

For some time, relations between the White House and Congress have been strained, in foreign policy no less than in many areas of domestic policy, even beyond the natural competition between the branches. You have an opportunity to "turn the page" and develop a new relationship with Congress. This is not just a call for greater civility in public life in Washington, nor is it an effort to blunt partisanship; despite the old adage that "politics stops at the water's edge," too much of foreign policy is inextricably mixed with domestic issues and concerns to be separated out and preserved from partisan debate. The question is the limits—and the overall atmosphere within which Executive-Legislative relations are conducted.

"Bipartisanship" in foreign policy should be a priority, even if it cannot always be attained. And leadership begins with you, as the official who, in law and in practice, has the most authority and capacity for initiative. Indeed, we believe that a primary rule of presidential leadership in foreign policy should be to build congressional and popular support for whatever course of action you deem in the best interests of the country.

You could begin, soon after the election, by saying clearly that you seek a new partnership with Congress in foreign policy and national security—without, of course, giving up any of the prerogatives that accrue to any president. These words would be matched in deeds, beginning with presidential meetings, held regularly throughout your administration, with congressional leaders of both parties.

You might also ask for reciprocity, as a gesture of mutual good faith, in prompt Senate action on your nominees for senior offices in foreign policy and national security. To this end, you should ensure high credibility and "confirmability" for the appointees and be willing to sacrifice some partisan benefits—for example, in ambassadorial appointments based primarily on campaign contributions—in exchange for speed of Senate action.

Every department and agency engaged in foreign policy should keep Congress fully informed of plans and programs; the "default position" should be sharing too much information rather than too little. One step in this direction would be to strengthen the various legislative affairs offices and to ensure that they work closely with the relevant substantive offices. You should also consider how to engage members of Congress in aspects of diplomacy that will lead to congressional (especially Senate) requirements for action. This might include exploring with congressional leaders areas where institutional partnerships can be created, patterned on the successful Legislative-Executive Commission on Security and Cooperation in Europe. And when the United States is engaged in major international negotiations that will lead to treaties subject to Senate ratification, you should, to the extent possible, invite congressional observers to be involved.

Finally, early in your administration, you should consider submitting to Congress an integrated "foreign policy and national security budget," to accompany the annual foreign policy report that is already required, along the lines of the annual consolidated budget and economic report. The budget and report should include explanations of connections, choices, and tradeoffs among different instruments of foreign policy and national security. While providing greater understanding in Congress of your overall goals, these submissions could also form the backdrop for broadening the policy dialogue between the administration and Congress—as well as fostering consideration of budget priorities, especially on the nonmilitary resources needed to sustain and advance U.S. foreign policy.

It is our judgment that, in this new age, the demands on the United States for diplomacy and other nonmilitary involvement abroad will rise significantly, for all of the reasons set forth in our basic analysis above regarding the challenges and opportunities now facing the nation, including efforts to reduce the risks of conflict and the need for engagement of U.S. forces. We thus believe that nonmilitary spending on foreign policy and national security (the so-called "150

Account") should be increased substantially, by at least 20 percent over current levels. But to achieve this, the Congress must be presented with a clear rationale; be convinced that diplomatic structures—especially the State Department—are being reformed, modernized, and made fully relevant to tomorrow's needs; and be drawn fully into your confidence about the requirements and the means of U.S. leadership and actions abroad. This can best be achieved by presenting an integrated policy and budget request and creating a sustained dialogue on broad national strategy.

ISSUES FOR IMMEDIATE DECISION

First Public Presentations

Your first public presentations after the election are important in creating a firm basis for leadership, doubly so because few of these issues have figured in the presidential campaign. At your first press conference during the transition, we suggest that you begin by publicly setting the foreign policy directions for your administration; this would include statements of reassurance about U.S. engagement abroad, which the allies, in particular, are always anxious to hear from a newly elected U.S. president. The following are the themes we recommend:

1. You will be active in leading the United States in the world. You are assembling a first-rate team with an international outlook to promote U.S. strength at home and U.S. interests and values abroad; the two will always go together in your administration.

2. Until January 20, Bill Clinton remains president and commander-in-chief, with the authority of his office for foreign policy and national security. You respect that role and support his exercise of his responsibility. No one should be in any doubt that President Clinton has the full powers of action during this transition period. You also want to make clear to everyone abroad that, unless and until you make changes after you become president, all of America's commitments remain firm and unaltered.

3. You are deeply committed to creating a new relationship with Congress; there has been too much division and discord in recent years. In foreign policy and national security, building

American strength and purpose in this era demands a partnership between the president and Congress. The American people expect that of all their leaders in Washington, and you will do your part to make this happen.

4. Maintaining a strong economy at home is critical to being strong and able to lead abroad. You will also continue to lead in ensuring the effective workings of the global financial system and an open trading system.

5. America's alliances and partnerships will have your concentrated support and attention, from Europe to Asia, with Japan and others. You will place a high priority on strengthening these relationships, which will be at the core of U.S. security and economic policy, also reaching out to other regions, such as Africa.

6. The United States will continue to be deeply committed both to NATO and to U.S. relations with the EU. You continue to support NATO enlargement, but you will make precise decisions for the United States later. You will review U.S. policy toward the Balkans, but changes, if any, will be made only in concert with the NATO allies.

7. You will be deeply engaged in developing effective long-term policies toward Russia, China, South Asia, Latin America, the Persian Gulf, and other areas critical to America's future; it would be premature to lay out policies at this point, however.

8. You are committed to help Israel obtain peace with all of its neighbors and to Israel's security; there should be no doubt about that. You expect to be actively involved. You will decide the precise terms and timing of U.S. engagement in peace negotiations after the inauguration and in light of circumstances, including possibilities for advancing the peace process.

9. You are already becoming engaged personally in the crafting of the defense budget and policy, including the Quadrennial Defense Review (QDR) that is now under way. America's defenses will be tailored to the needs of the future; they will honor America's fighting men and women; and they will keep the nation secure and make the American people proud. Within the overall review, you will direct a fundamental analysis of all the factors in missile defenses, including the decision on National Missile

Defense (NMD) postponed by President Clinton. You are committed to missile defense to protect the United States, its troops, and its allies, and you will ensure that the nation gets this right, in all dimensions; but you cannot now foreshadow the outcome of your analysis.

10. You will mandate, immediately upon assuming office, a root-and-branch review of U.S. foreign and national security policy, the first such in-depth review since the end of the Cold War and long overdue. This will include all the classic concerns of the United States, but also newer concerns, including WMD, terrorism, and globalization, as well as issues such as democracy, poverty, and human rights.

Critical Decisions

As the new U.S. president, you will be accorded a grace period by the nation and much of the world in making basic decisions on U.S. foreign and defense policy. However, we believe that in several areas you will rapidly need at least to prepare for reaching decisions with long-range implications. These decisions relate to issues that either were in abeyance near the end of the current administration, are driven by external developments, or relate to your ability to shape major budget choices for Fiscal Year 2002. We have singled out three: missile defense, reshaping the defense program, and the Arab-Israeli peace process.

Missile Defense. The missile defense issue will be among the most critical for your administration. Indeed, mishandling this issue could have severe consequences across a wide range of concerns, including the nation's military security and relations with the allies, Russia, and China. On September 1, President Clinton postponed basic decisions on National Missile Defense (NMD) until the next administration, saying, "I simply cannot conclude with the information I have today that we have enough confidence in the technology, and the operational effectiveness of the entire NMD system, to move forward to deployment."

Within the membership of the Transition 2001 panel, there is a basic agreement that creating an effective NMD capability is part of an overall strategy not only of protecting the United States against a limited ballistic-missile attack, but also of ensuring that it will continue to be able to project conventional military power credibly, even against threats from a state armed with a limited number of ballistic missiles and nuclear, biological, or chemical warheads. We also agree on the importance of developing and deploying effective theater missile-defense (TMD) systems in key locations around the world—perhaps combining boost-phase intercept with midcourse and terminal defense—and we agree on the need for reductions of strategic nuclear weapons, whether by treaty or unilaterally. Within the panel, however, opinions vary considerably about the best way to move forward with NMD. We do concur that plans for NMD deserve a fresh look and that this issue should be accorded the highest priority within your administration and in national discussion and debate. We suggest that, promptly after inauguration, you lay the groundwork for making basic decisions.

You should consider leading a comprehensive effort, as part of a broader review of issues of military defense, nonproliferation, strategic stability, and diplomatic relations. Among the most important elements of this comprehensive effort would be the following:

- A review by the intelligence community of emerging long-range threats posed by states such as North Korea, Iran, and Iraq, including the likely timelines for their appearance and an assessment of the prospects for avoiding them via diplomatic agreement (e.g., a possible deal with North Korea).

- Assessment of different NMD alternatives (including combination or layering of different alternatives) in light of the source and nature of emergent threats, U.S. technical capabilities, probability of mission success (including effectiveness against expected countermeasures), cost-effectiveness, areas of coverage (including allies and friends), and time of availability.

- Assessment of alternative or complementary means of dealing with emerging long-range missile threats, including denial of capabilities, diplomacy, deterrence, and preemptive action.

- Assessment of the relationship of different NMD alternatives to the ABM Treaty, the possibilities for withdrawing from the treaty or reaching an understanding with Russia for altering it, and the potential impact of either option.

- Assessment of the impact that missile defense programs could have on the funding of other U.S. military programs, including impacts on the pace and timing of development and deployment.

- Diplomacy with allies regarding the full range of issues, including threat assessment, alternative and complementary responses, the impact on relations with countries such as Russia and China, incentives for other countries to support U.S. missile defense plans, and/or possible accommodation to those plans, and adjustment in U.S. planning in response to allied concerns and suggestions.

There are several technological contenders for a U.S. NMD system, including the current land-based midcourse intercept system, boost-phase intercept systems, and some combination of air-based, space-based, and sea-based systems. Each has positive and negative attributes; any will involve tradeoffs among desirable objectives. The essential point for your decision is to evaluate each of these possibilities in light of the complex considerations discussed above and to embed your decision in broader policy deliberations. Because of the high costs involved, the many issues at stake, and the controversy—both at home and abroad—that will attend any choice, it is critical to get this decision as "right" as possible and to take sufficient time in doing so.

Whatever choice you make, you should also build a base of support within Congress; and you should use the entire process to develop a widespread sense within the country that overall U.S. security and foreign policy objectives have been served. To this end, creating a process for analysis and decision can enable you to consider a full range of options, factor in all the critical elements, and exercise leadership in building support, both at home and abroad.

Reshaping the Defense Program. Like your predecessors, you will need to make some of the most consequential decisions regarding U.S. defense and military forces during the first six to nine months of your administration—perhaps even before your new Pentagon team is fully in place. What you decide in these few, rather frenetic months will go far toward shaping the U.S. military posture for the balance of your administration and beyond.

For you to exercise leadership, we recommend that you and your defense team undertake four major sets of activities, more or less in parallel:

- *Strategy development.* To provide a sound basis for every other defense decision, your administration should develop, even if at first in rudimentary form, an overall concept of national security strategy that includes the most important military, economic, and diplomatic dimensions. This will provide the foundation for the formal National Security Strategy document mandated by Congress. In the process, you should begin confronting some basic defense policy choices, even if you do not immediately resolve them, such as whether to continue adhering to the doctrine of the United States being prepared to conduct two nearly simultaneous major theater wars (MTWs) as the primary criterion for force-sizing.

- *Alterations to the Fiscal Year 2002 budget submission.* You will inherit from the current administration a draft defense budget that, as a practical matter, must be submitted to Congress by April. Because of its size, complexity, and state of development, you and your defense team will not be able to review it in any detail, and it will be difficult to make radical changes. Thus, you should consider focusing on its key provisions to determine that they are consistent with the overall thrust of your defense strategy. You may also wish to highlight policy shifts by proposing one or more high-profile changes to the submission.

- *Producing your own defense program—the QDR.* The congressionally mandated QDR must be completed by the end of September. The purpose of the QDR is to articulate a defense strategy (i.e., the military component of your national security strategy) and to produce an affordable defense program that will yield the capabilities needed to execute that strategy. The QDR should thus be produced in tandem with your basic national security strategy review and alterations to the Fiscal Year 2002 budget submission.

- *Signaling your intentions to allies (and others).* Your new administration's deliberations about its defense program and posture will be closely scrutinized by allies, friends, and adversaries. We suggest that, early on, you send some clear signals about your intentions (e.g., whether you plan any changes in the pattern and character of U.S. force deployments abroad), preferably without locking yourself into positions that might later need to be revised.

You will not, however, be starting with a clean slate. There is great momentum (some would say inertia) behind every major component of the defense program, and the Pentagon has been working for months on position papers, options, and analyses intended to present your new administration with available choices. Left on "autopilot," this process is quite capable of building a program and carrying it out without direction by you or your new defense team. But such a "business as usual" approach would be likely to avoid the tough questions, thus producing a total defense structure that is more costly than necessary.

Your administration will face many significant challenges in ensuring that U.S. military forces are able to meet the needs of the nation for the years ahead. But the chief problems that your new Secretary of Defense must confront all stem from the fact that for about the past ten years, the Department of Defense has, unwittingly but consistently, underestimated the cost of maintaining and operating its force structure. This has led to the following problems, which are becoming increasingly acute:

- Training opportunities have been reduced, and some accounts for spare parts and equipment maintenance have been starved, leading to sinking in-commission rates, more man-hours required for routine maintenance, and a consequent decline in morale and readiness.

- Programs to provide important new capabilities (e.g., a new generation of surveillance sensors, advanced munitions, TMD) have been delayed.

- More prosaic accounts, such as military housing and real property maintenance, have suffered, leading to a deterioration of the physical plant at many bases.

The severity of these problems is magnified by the fact that much of the force faces significant new charges to modernize or recapitalize the weapon and support platforms that were fielded in the 1970s and

1980s. Current U.S. strategy now demands capabilities (e.g., stealth) that old platforms simply cannot provide. Thus, a sizable modernization bill cannot be avoided. As a result, the first and most important job of your new Secretary of Defense will be to build and execute an affordable defense program that is balanced over the longer term. This means putting enough resources into the chronically underfunded accounts so that near-term readiness does not suffer unduly, while providing as well for the future with modernization spending that keeps ahead of the obsolescence "bow-wave." Striking this balance—the near term versus the long term—is one of the most important national defense program and policy tasks facing the U.S. military and your administration.

Experts differ on the exact cost of providing for adequate U.S. defenses over the next several years. A reasonable estimate, however, is that, without changes in other areas, the Department of Defense will need an increase of about $30 billion per year in the procurement accounts, and an additional $10 billion per year for real property maintenance, recruitment, pay and retirement, medical care, and the like. In all, this represents an after-inflation defense budget increase of at least 10 percent, sustained over many years.

The need for increased funding means that something must change in the underlying demands for resources within the Department of Defense program. The current U.S. strategy places heavy demands on our forces in peacetime and in conflict. Unless you change this strategy, cutting force structure may not be prudent. That said, we believe that with modification of the current strategy, cuts can be made, in part by introducing more modern and more capable systems and forces. Resources can also be saved over the long term by rationalizing the military base structure in the United States and adopting more effective business practices. Making such changes happen will involve some difficult and controversial decisions, and your best opportunity for overcoming resistance will come during the administration's first year. This underscores the importance of producing a QDR that reflects key priorities and shapes basic decisions.

Past reviews have tended to ratify the status quo and have usually failed to address requirements for change. Experience suggests several lessons for increasing the chances that your administration can exercise command. Chief among these lessons are the following:

- *Change must come from the top.* You should empower the Secretary of Defense to make major changes in the allocation of resources. Extensive consultation within the Department of Defense and with Congress will be essential. In the end, however, you must be prepared to spend political capital in order to make any major reallocation of defense resources.

- *Expand the range of scenarios used to evaluate future U.S. military forces.* The two basic, stylized scenarios used for most of the military's force evaluation today (a North Korean attack on South Korea and an Iraqi attack on Kuwait and Saudi Arabia) do not in themselves constitute an adequate yardstick for assessing capabilities needed in the future. U.S. forces might become engaged in entirely different contexts, including ones that involve more-modern forces than North Korea or Iraq can field or that involve less warning or non–armored-invasion threats—such as light forces or amphibious invasions supported by large numbers of ballistic and cruise missiles.

- *Understand that "the system" will provide options and supporting analyses that discount qualitative improvements in weaponry.* Most of the analytical tools used by the Department of Defense were developed prior to recent advances in information and precision technologies, and therefore they have difficulty reflecting the value of such innovations for military capabilities. Your new Secretary of Defense must take the initiative to ensure the introduction of better, higher-fidelity analyses into the deliberative process.

The Arab-Israeli Peace Process. For the past 30 years, the United States has played the leading external role in promoting Arab-Israeli peace, and its commitments—both to peace and to Israel's security—remain firm. Successive administrations—and presidents—have thus expended considerable time, effort, and political and financial capital on Arab-Israeli diplomacy. Indeed, President Clinton raised the level of U.S. and direct presidential involvement. His active engagement at the July 2000 Camp David Summit broke new ground on issues, including Jerusalem, which had previously been taboo, effectively reducing the option of making Arab-Israeli peace negotiations a second-order priority for your administration.

The recent breakdown of the peace process and the ensuing violence have intensified levels of distrust among both Israelis and Palestinians, raised questions about the continued viability of the Oslo framework, and sparked concern about regression in wider Arab-Israeli relations and even the potential for regional conflict. Indeed, it is possible that the beginning of your presidency will be marked by continued fighting in the Middle East, imposing the requirement of U.S. efforts to bring the violence to a halt as a prerequisite for any further attempts at making a lasting peace.

It is not clear whether Yassir Arafat could again be a credible peace partner for Israel, whether Israeli politics would soon be amenable to a renewal of the peace process, or whether possible leadership changes on the Palestinian or the Israeli side would affect the potential for diplomacy. Nevertheless, all parties look to you, as the U.S. president, to play a critical role. As your administration begins, you will need to judge whether the political temper in the area could support an early resumption of high-level diplomacy or whether more time and perhaps concrete acts of confidence-building are first required. More fundamentally, you will need to judge how seriously the fall 2000 violence threatens to deteriorate into a wider crisis that could threaten U.S. and allied interests, and you will need to decide what to do to prevent escalation and restore the prospects for diplomacy. On the Israeli-Palestinian front itself, you will need to decide whether to pick up where President Clinton left off—that is, to try resuming an active role in diplomacy on the basis of the Oslo/Camp David framework; to pursue a less-ambitious, modified version; or to explore alternative approaches.

Thus, you will have key decisions to make about how negotiations and other diplomatic activity should be conducted, as well as about possible requirements for dealing with ongoing violence. These decisions include whether you should take the initiative or wait until the parties signal willingness to resume negotiations, whether you want to appoint a special negotiator or center diplomacy with the Secretary of State and his or her subordinates, and what your personal role, if any, will be. You should consider directing an internal assessment of the potential for proceeding with the Camp David approach versus pursuing alternative ways to achieve an Israeli-Palestinian "final status agreement," such as a return to step-by-step diplomacy or the adoption of an alternative strategy of disengagement and "separation." More widely, in working to prevent a worsening of the regional situation and in approaching a resumption of a U.S. role in negotiations, it makes sense to place emphasis on securing the support of key European allies and major Arab states, particularly Egypt and Saudi Arabia, both for the peace process and for the U.S. role in it.

Early in your administration, you should consider making clear publicly your basic approaches, even if you reserve your options—for example, whether the United States should take the initiative or wait to respond, and whether you should play a direct role from the beginning or reserve intense, active involvement for when it is needed to help the parties either to reach closure or to avert a breakdown in the process.

We recommend that you make clear the following:

- The United States is prepared, actively and vigorously, to support efforts to reach peace between Israel and its neighbors, building on what has been achieved in the past. But the circumstances have to be such that there is a basis for a viable peace process and an absence of violence.

- U.S. commitments, particularly security commitments to Israel, remain firm, unquestioned, and unlinked to this diplomacy.

- U.S. engagement can take place only on the basis of the firm commitment of all parties to the peaceful resolution of conflict, and the United States opposes unilateral acts outside the scope of negotiations that could damage prospects for peace.

- You are ready to assign a first-class team to advance the goal of Arab-Israeli peace when the timing is appropriate. As with all U.S. diplomacy, the Secretary of State will have overall direction, under your guidance.

- If the parties do support resumption of the peace process, as it develops, you will determine the appropriate level of your own engagement in diplomacy.

- Your commitment is clear: to continue the active role of the United States in creating a just and lasting peace between Israel and all of its neighbors and in engaging the entire region in the great promise of the global economy.

POSSIBLE CRISES AND OPPORTUNITIES

Between your election and inauguration, it is likely that one or more foreign crises will occur that require some form of action by the United States. This is, of course, a sensitive period, when the outgoing president must make decisions, but the incoming president has to live with the results. This works best when the departing president draws his successor into his confidence—and even seeks his advice, while recognizing that the "buck (still) stops here." Your staff and that of President Clinton should consult promptly after the election to ensure that you are at least kept fully informed and also to develop transition arrangements that will best provide for continuity and the protection of national interests at the time of changing administrations.

By the same token, we suggest that, in organizing your administration, you place high priority on developing your basic crisis management team. That should begin with your top officials who are not subject to Senate confirmation, centering on your new National Security Advisor. In the event of a crisis just after your inauguration, you should also be able to draw on counsel from your designees for cabinet positions in foreign policy and national security, even if they have not yet been confirmed. We recommend that before doing so, however, you consult with the Senate leadership; it is unlikely that in a crisis, your making use of these appointees would be objected to. In any event, you should have in place a streamlined team of crisis managers, chaired on your behalf by the National Security Advisor, as soon as possible after inauguration.

Iraq

At the beginning of the Clinton administration, Saddam Hussein sought to challenge the new president by provoking a crisis in the Persian Gulf. He may do the same to you; and even without a crisis, you will face a difficult situation in Iraq. Saddam Hussein refuses to allow inspectors to assess his compliance with United Nations (UN) resolutions on WMD. At the same time, international support for sanctions and U.S. Iraqi policy in general has declined. The United States has declared its goal of changing the regime in Baghdad but has not yet developed a viable strategy for doing so.

In forcing an early crisis, Saddam could step up his efforts to shoot down U.S. aircraft enforcing the no-fly zones, move his forces into the autonomous Kurdish areas in support of one Kurdish faction, threaten Kuwait, or continue efforts to manipulate the oil market by reducing or stopping Iraqi oil exports. How you respond to such challenges will shape not only Saddam's future actions, but also those of others in the Middle East. It will also have an impact on long-term U.S. goals, including peace between Israel and the Arabs, limiting the proliferation of WMD, and the security of the oil-rich states.

We recommend that your short-term strategy in responding to Iraqi actions adhere to the following principles:

- If provoked, U.S. air attacks on Iraq should hit a wider range of strategic and military targets. Current U.S. strikes on air defense systems accomplish relatively little. As long as you are willing to pay the political and operational costs of a continued military campaign against Iraq, the campaign should be directed against targets that count: the forces of elite units, regime-protection assets, and suspected WMD sites.

- The potential operational, diplomatic, and other risks of such attacks argue for rapid analysis of the situation you inherit, consideration of alternatives, and decisions about the key elements of an overall policy. In few, if any, other areas of foreign policy is the development of contingency plans rooted in a longer-term strategy more necessary at the outset of your administration.

- The United States should continue its leadership in the struggle against Iraq, but it should be recognized that unless you are prepared to act unilaterally, exercising this leadership will require some accommodation to allied reactions and interests. For example, it will be easier to lead both U.S. regional and global allies in response to an Iraqi threat to Kuwait than to a move by Saddam against the Kurds. You should communicate early your determination to protect U.S. redlines—on WMD, on threats to Kuwait or other U.S. allies, and on interference in the Kurdish areas. If you decide, for example, that Iraq must be prevented from making any substantial progress with any of its WMD programs, you must be prepared to act if credible intelligence indicates such progress. You would also need to demonstrate that U.S. actions in Iraq are directed against the regime and to discourage, to the extent possible, divisions among partners that encourage Saddam to take hostile action or that complicate responses to that action.

- The United States and other Western states should, in any event, prepare for the possibility of temporary reductions in Iraqi oil exports. You should consider an agreement with our allies that in the event of an Iraqi-inspired oil crisis, we will all draw on strategic reserves until other producers can replace as much of the shortfall as possible. Your preparations should include efforts to reach a prior agreement with Saudi Arabia, which has the largest excess production capacity.

- The UN must retain control over Iraqi spending, the main lever for keeping Saddam Hussein from rebuilding his conventional forces and expanding his WMD. By the same token, you should consult with partners and other states about the current sanctions and about changes that could make them more sustainable and more effective for achieving U.S. and allied interests. You should also consider changes that would allow increasing contacts between the Iraqi people and the outside world and an increased Iraqi capacity for oil production.

China and Taiwan

Critical differences between Mainland China and Taiwan about the future of their relations make the Taiwan issue the most intractable and dangerous East Asian flashpoint—and the one with the greatest potential for bringing the United States and China into confrontation in the near future. The Chinese leadership still has not fully decided on its response to the March 2000 election in Taiwan of an independence-oriented president from the Democratic Progressive Party (DPP). That election sparked renewed fears in Beijing that Taiwan is drifting toward independence and prompted Beijing to reiterate its threats to use force to prevent Taiwan from achieving *de jure* independence. China now asserts that even Taiwan's refusal to negotiate "*sine die*" on reunification might force it "to adopt all drastic measures possible, including the use of force, to safeguard China's sovereignty and territorial integrity."

Any of several apparently minor developments could upset the delicate status quo in the Taiwan Strait and generate a crisis. Of particular concern is the possibility that a crisis might evolve before your administration has a chance to articulate a coherent policy regarding Taiwan. Even without a deliberate move toward independence, the ordinary workings of Taiwan's dynamic democracy could produce words or deeds that would appear provocative to Beijing. If the Taiwanese and Mainland Chinese have different or inaccurate understandings of how the new U.S. administration would react to such a crisis, the situation might quickly spiral out of control.

China's military weakness, the ambiguous U.S. commitment to protect Taiwan against aggression, and Taiwan's own defense forces ought to suffice to deter Beijing from outright invasion for the next several years. But because of the emotional and nationalist element in Beijing's attitudes toward Taiwan, this assumption could prove unrealistic. Moreover, Chinese military options are not limited to an outright invasion but could entail harassment of Taiwanese shipping at sea, missile attacks on Taiwanese targets, or a forceful quarantine of the island's ports. Rather than conquer the island by main force, such attacks would be intended to panic the Taiwanese and, by raising the costs of refusal, coerce them into making a reunification deal on Beijing's terms.

Such a campaign would threaten not only Taiwan, but also U.S. political and economic interests in East Asia. Chinese action against Taiwan would also present a military dilemma for your administration. If the United States stood aside, its credibility in East Asia as a guarantor of stability would be severely damaged. If, on the other hand, the United States did intervene, it might damage—severely and perhaps for the long term—the important economic and diplomatic relationship with China, possibly setting the stage for a new Cold War with the world's most important rising power. And, of course, any Sino-U.S. confrontation would play out in the long shadow of the two sides' intercontinental nuclear arsenals.

Your ability to respond to such a campaign has clear limits—e.g., the United States can currently offer Taiwan little effective protection against Chinese ballistic missiles. While U.S. air and naval forces could help ensure freedom of navigation for all shipping through international waters, such an operation would need to be carefully managed to minimize the chances of a shooting war through misjudgment or mischance. Maintaining this type of response could require a sustained commitment and could become a dangerous showdown.

Attempting to avoid such a confrontation should be a top priority for your administration. You will need to decide whether to maintain the current policy of "constructive ambiguity"—accepting the principle of "One China" while simultaneously providing nonspecific assurances regarding Taiwan's defense—or instead to adopt a clearer policy that fosters greater confidence that all parties know where the United States stands. Such a policy would have two central features:

- It would reiterate to both sides that the United States firmly opposes any unilateral moves toward independence by Taiwan but will also support Taiwan in the event of an unprovoked Chinese attack.

- It would reiterate that the United States has a commitment to fostering Taiwan's economy and democratic way of life but also wishes to maintain strong, positive, and friendly relations with China.

In the event of a crisis between China and Taiwan, the primary U.S. goal should be to defuse the situation as quickly as possible. To this end, the United States could share intelligence information with both sides to help decisionmakers in Beijing and Taipei maintain an accurate picture of the situation and simultaneously to demonstrate the impossibility of achieving operational or tactical surprise. The United States should also make its intentions known early in any crisis. Particularly in the event of an actual or apparently imminent Chinese use of force, prompt and public force movements and firm statements of U.S. support for Taiwan might cause the Chinese to at least refrain from further escalating tensions.

The Korean Opportunity

Early in your administration, you could face either a crisis or an opportunity on the Korean peninsula. At this point, a breakthrough in diplomacy appears to be in the offing. While resolution of this last-remaining Cold War conflict would be a welcome development, it would also have important effects on the long-term U.S. goal of maintaining stability in East Asia as a whole. Even if the Korean conflict is resolved, that goal will require a strong and well-configured U.S. military presence in the region and ultimately a web of regional security arrangements. This is fully expected by America's allies and friends in Asia, as part of the major transition in power and economic relationships that is likely to take place during the next several years.

Prompt and coherent U.S. action early in the process of a breakthrough on the Korean peninsula could promote these long-term goals, building on what has been achieved in late 2000, while at the same time helping to assure a smooth and peaceful transition in Korea. Early in your administration, therefore, the United States needs to have a coherent strategy ready to deploy. This strategy should have the following features:

- Resolution of the Korean dispute is essentially an intra-Korean issue to be solved by the two countries. While pursuing changes in North Korean policy, especially in regard to U.S. concerns about nuclear and other critical military issues, the United States should not interfere in sensitive North-South negotiations where its presence might only complicate matters. The United States should also ensure that the South Koreans are fully informed of all U.S. contacts with North Korea and that they have no cause for concern that the United States is dealing with the North behind their backs. (Achieving such a split between South Korea and the United States has been a long-term North Korean goal.) Consistent with this policy, the United States should deploy its diplomatic resources to protect the negotiations from complications that might be introduced by other regional powers.

- At the same time, the United States has some critical interests that should be succinctly communicated to the South Korean government prior to any serious negotiations with the North. These conditions fall into two categories. First, the United States should underscore its desire that any WMD and ballistic-missile programs currently existing in the North be terminated. Second, the United States should communicate the benefits of moving North Korea away from the idea of building nuclear power plants and toward alternative energy sources. Finally, the United States should seek a prior agreement with Seoul on the basic outlines of the U.S. force posture that will continue to be deployed in Korea after a breakthrough. The United States does not need a military presence in the North and would reduce its troop presence in the South, reflecting the fact that the U.S. mission would change from deterring aggression to promoting regional stability. This military reduction would also most likely involve a change in the types of forces deployed, reducing the number of ground troops and retaining relatively more air, naval, and logistics assets.

- In exchange, the United States would include the Korean peninsula, under any political arrangement the Koreans themselves should agree upon, beneath the U.S. security umbrella and would guarantee the security and independence of the peninsula. The United States would also provide economic assistance on both a multilateral and a bilateral basis, in order to help integrate the North Korean economy and society with the South.

- Any changes to the basic U.S. posture on the Korean peninsula should also be fully coordinated with our other regional allies, especially Japan, and in consultation with China.

Despite current optimism, there could still be a sudden reversion by the regime in Pyongyang to a more confrontational, isolationist posture. While that is not now likely, the United States should keep in place the policies, positions, and forces that would be needed to respond.

Colombia

Early in your administration, you could confront a crisis in Colombia stemming from the Colombian government's loss of control over large parts of the country, as well as general instability. Such a development could cause a spillover of Colombia's problems into other parts of the Andean region, threatening stability throughout Latin America.

Instability in Colombia results from three interactive factors: the social and economic inequities prevailing in Colombian society, the underground drug economy, and the growth of armed challenges to state authority by groups such as the Marxist Revolutionary Armed Forces of Colombia (FARC). This situation has created a major security problem, both for the immediate region and for the United States. The United States already provides significant assistance to the Colombian government. In July 2000, the U.S. Congress approved an emergency supplemental counternarcotics package of $1.3 billion for the Andean region, of which $862 million was allocated to support the Colombian government's Plan Colombia. However, the bulk of the assistance—Blackhawk helicopters for three new counternarcotics battalions—is not scheduled to be delivered for another six months to a year. The situation remains dire, with significant implications for the stability of the Andean region and the capacity of the United States to reduce the drug trade.

To test your resolve, the FARC might take one of the following steps: attack U.S. or U.S.-contracted aircraft used to support the Colombian's coca and poppy eradication missions; conduct major attacks against and even defeat Colombian army units; or carry out a spectacular attack on Bogotá or other major Colombian cities. An escalating crisis in Colombia could confront the United States with two unattractive alternatives: to abandon its counternarcotics and regional stability interests or to become more deeply involved in a protracted internal conflict. To try to avoid such a choice, the United States needs a coherent Colombian strategy in place early in your administration. We recommend that this strategy have three central goals:

- *To assist the democratic and friendly Colombian government.* The United States should rapidly provide additional equipment, such as transport and attack helicopters, reconnaissance assets, and communications equipment, and should help the Colombians develop intelligence collection and dissemination. Over the longer term, the Colombian Army will need U.S. assistance to increase its rapid-reaction capabilities. But U.S. involvement should exclude the involvement of American troops in military operations.

- *To develop a web of cooperation with concerned Latin American states, such as Panama, Brazil, and Ecuador, to deal with the Colombian crisis and to help promote regional stability over the longer term.* Regional leaders expect this effort from the United States, which is uniquely capable of providing it. Panama has become a key node in the Colombian narco-traffickers' and guerrillas' support structure. Ecuador is already the victim of cross-border raids from Colombia. To shut down the narco-traffickers' and guerrillas' pipeline, Panamanian security forces will need to be strengthened, and Ecuador will need to reinforce its borders with Colombia. Given Brazil's extensive border with Colombia, it should also play a central role in a regional strategy.

- *To use these regional relations to assist in containing and weakening the Colombian narco-traffickers and guerrillas.*

At the same time, we suggest that you fully engage the U.S. Congress in planning and carrying out your Colombian strategy. Because of the potential risks of being drawn in too deeply, U.S. engagement should be undertaken only under circumstances in which you can count on strong public and congressional backing. One means of attaining this support is to acknowledge that the risks that Colombia poses to regional stability in Latin America and U.S. interests in general justify treating Colombia not just as an extension of the war against drugs, but also as a national security issue.

Chapter Three

SETTING THE STAGE: LONGER-TERM ISSUES

Most of this report has been about that steps we believe you should take either during the transition or soon after inauguration to help you exercise leadership on a limited but critical range of issues, including crises, that you could face quite quickly. At the same time, there are several areas in which we believe you should begin quite early in your administration to set directions for the country abroad, even though what you do now might not come to fruition for several years. More particularly, there are areas where, in our judgment, if you want to have a critical impact on future developments, you will need to start building the basis for action during the first few months after you become president. We recognize that this will not always be easy. It is especially challenging for any president to try focusing national attention on developments that are some distance off in the future; equally important, it is not always easy to expend the needed political capital or national resources. But, in some cases, it is important to make the effort in the long-term interests of the nation.

We have also chosen not to present you with a "laundry list"—a comprehensive compilation of issues and approaches covering all parts of the world and all functional questions. Instead, we have singled out a few that we believe to be particularly consequential, either in terms of world developments or in terms of the U.S. role, and on which what you do in the first year can have a particularly important impact.

DEFENSE ISSUES: SUSTAINING A PREEMINENT MILITARY

Even in the absence of a superpower rival, U.S. military strength remains a critical component of U.S. power, influence, and position in the world. The United States uniquely has the ability to project military power and sustain it over long distances. It is this capability that underpins all U.S. alliance and security commitments. The United States thus needs military forces strong enough to play a critical role in shaping the security environment, to deter challenges to our interests, and therefore to reduce the likelihood of conflict. And if conflict should occur, our military must be able to achieve rapid and decisive victory against a wide range of potential adversaries—both state and nonstate actors.

Our armed forces face many challenges. While we are clearly the preeminent military power in the world today, the missions assigned to U.S. forces are inherently demanding. Fighting and winning wars, whether large or small, in other nations' "back yards" has never been easy. With the proliferation of longer-range, more-lethal attack systems into the hands of regional adversaries, such expeditionary operations are becoming more challenging. The challenge is complicated by the fact that an enemy generally chooses the time and place of the initial attack. Since U.S. forces cannot be routinely deployed everywhere in large numbers, this puts a premium on forces that can deploy quickly to theaters where conflict is occurring and that can quickly seize the initiative. In addition, in order to sustain support, both at home and in coalitions with allies, costs and risks of military operations must be kept proportionate to the interests at stake. This requirement increases the complexity of conducting military operations.

To meet these requirements, we also need to overcome some looming problems in the military to ensure that it remains ready to meet current challenges and can take particular advantage of emerging technologies. Our military forces are facing the progressive obsolescence of many of their premier platforms. Operating costs of current forces are high and growing, and force deployments (often unplanned) for peacekeeping and humanitarian purposes have imposed significant burdens. Signs of strain include shortfalls in meeting recruiting goals, losses of experienced personnel, and in some cases, declining morale. Despite the recent increase in the defense budget, a gap remains between available resources and the demands of the current strategy.

But these worrisome trends also present an opportunity. The strengthening of the U.S. military should take place in the context of a long-delayed transformation of American security strategy and defense posture. Indeed, by and large, we are still living with a defense establishment that was a legacy of the Cold War. This is the time to move aggressively to develop and field systems that can underwrite new ways of conducting military operations. We have had glimpses of the future: sensors that can detect moving vehicles over huge sections of the battlefield day or night and in all weather, and guided munitions that give our forces precision attack capabilities in all weather conditions.

Thus, the most important tasks for your administration in its next defense review are to recommend a force posture that will make U.S. strategy and defense resources compatible and to devise a system for monitoring whether those resources are allocated strategically before signs of wear and tear emerge. Without measures along these lines, mismatches between resources and requirements, between rhetoric and reality, and between opportunity and accomplishment will likely continue.

During the Cold War, the Soviet threat provided a central focus for planning and force development. Today, our strategy must balance the American security portfolio against a wider range of possibilities, both geographically and functionally. Thus, the United States must move away from reliance on point solutions to fielding a force that can handle diverse problems, such as attacks involving the use of missiles and WMD, as well as attacks against U.S. information systems. Moreover, U.S. forces must have specialized capabilities for smaller-scale operations, such as interventions, peacekeeping, and humanitarian operations, which, while generally less critical to the national interest than major wars, are likely to remain principal missions of the military. At the same time, the budgeting process must accept that such crisis response operations will interfere with long-term military development plans if they are not funded adequately. Your administration must find ways to fund those operations that minimize disruptions to other important military programs and activities.

The need to handle new types of missions will put a premium on deciding upon the appropriate role of institutions outside the military in meeting these challenges. This includes deciding how the Intelligence community should focus its efforts and what capabilities not assigned by default to the armed forces (e.g., post-conflict law enforcement and civil administration, or drug interdiction) should be provided by other agencies.

Your administration also needs to determine the extent to which we can count on our allies in meeting the diverse range of future military challenges. U.S. allies' capabilities should be more effectively integrated into U.S. force planning in order to achieve greater interoperability and to relieve some of the burdens on U.S. resources. For political as well as economic reasons, the United States needs to encourage its allies both to increase their capability for power projection and to be more effective in coalition with U.S. forces. At times, the U.S. government has been ambivalent about increasing allied capabilities and roles—especially about allowing its allies a greater decisionmaking role in military operations.

The U.S. government has also been reluctant to share high technology; this has hampered both interoperability and a transatlantic defense industry relationship that could benefit both sides. We believe you should propose far-reaching changes in the transatlantic regime for defense exports and investments, providing greater flexibility for countries and companies that agree to manage their own export control rules, compatible with U.S. practice. In the case of Japan, your administration should consider encouraging it gradually to revise its constitution to allow the right of collective self-defense, to expand its security horizon beyond territorial defense, and to acquire appropriate capabilities for supporting coalition operations. In Europe, U.S. policy should be to place greater priority on encouraging efforts at defense integration and rationalization across borders, while ensuring that NATO remains the central institution for transatlantic cooperation on European security.

Finally, your administration must find a way to continue recruiting and retaining the skilled personnel that are the most critical element of American military superiority. To deal with the recruitment and retention challenges posed by a booming economy, the Department of Defense will have to consider a variety of options: increase compensation across the board; overhaul the compensation system, targeting it at the most pressing problems; or restructure military ca-

reers. Some combination of all these options may be required.
RAND research shows that targeted compensation increases, especially those aimed at skilled enlisted personnel, produce better results than across-the-board increases. However, even targeted increases need to be supplemented by other tactics to increase the
flexibility of the military compensation system, so that it can respond
rapidly to changes in the civilian economy and in military personnel
requirements. Such tactics might include special bonuses to increase
retention of critical personnel, separation pay and tax-sheltered
retirement savings plans to allow more flexible retirement schedules,
and additional recruiting resources to attract new types of recruits.
At the same time, adjustments must be made in personnel policies to
ensure that serving men and women do not face a tempo of
operations that reduces their effectiveness, lowers their morale, and,
all too often, causes good people to leave the services when their
enlistments are up.

Defense Acquisition

The need for transformation applies just as much to the industrial
base that supports the U.S. military. During the Cold War, the U.S.
government evolved a development process for new weapons systems that proved highly successful. Central to success was harness-
ing the competitive energies of the private sector in both development and production of military systems. Private companies were
often motivated to subsidize development efforts with their own capital because the "production prize" the government promised was so
lucrative. Thanks to the ongoing long-term U.S. competition with
the Soviet Union, companies could look forward to frequent prize
awards.

The end of the Cold War and the "procurement holiday" that accom-
panied it have undercut key elements of this system. Not only are
the prizes much smaller, they are given much less frequently. It
should not be surprising that defense firms have sharply curtailed
their own investment in military research and development. Com-
plicating this challenge, the present trend toward defense industry
consolidation has led to a great concentration in virtually all defense
sectors, and competition in both development and production is
more difficult to achieve.

At the same time, some firms with potentially attractive technologies are reluctant to do business with the Department of Defense, complaining about the limited profitability of defense contracts, the threat that federal contract provisions pose to their intellectual property rights, and the costly process requirements associated with government business. In view of U.S. reliance on technology to create forces of superior capabilities, these are troubling developments.

We therefore recommend that you direct the Department of Defense to undertake four major reforms:

- First, reduce as much as possible the special administrative requirements of doing business with the Department of Defense. This will help current defense suppliers reduce overhead costs and make it easier for other companies to become defense suppliers.

- Second, increase design activity rates by facilitating some design and development programs without a full-scale production commitment—that is, increase the use of technology demonstrator programs and operational demonstrations. The first would focus on one or two design issues and would involve the fabrication of two platforms. The second would aim for development and operational testing and would involve a small production run (where the platforms were not fully engineered). If both government and the industry can make austere development more of a rule than an exception—and if Congress complies—it should be possible to double the number of design products for a 10 or 20 percent increase in the modernization budget.

- Third, make defense research and development contracts profitable in their own right, thereby removing an increasingly large barrier to entry and innovation and eliminating what is now a perverse incentive to move automatically—and sometimes prematurely or inappropriately—into production.

- Fourth, include reconstitution as an explicit pillar of national military strategy. To this end, the Department of Defense should try to maintain production of key systems at a low rate and should close down production lines in ways that make restarting production feasible in terms of difficulty, time, and cost.

Defense Infrastructure

Your administration will have a major opportunity to rationalize defense by restarting the base closure and realignment process. It is widely believed that the present set of bases is too large and thus too costly for the needs of the U.S. military.

Early in your administration, when the political costs are relatively low, you should consider seeking new authority from Congress to conduct further rounds of Base Realignment and Closure (BRAC). The model followed earlier is still probably best: an independent commission appointed to present to Congress a set of changes that must be decided as a package. The commission may consider recommendations from both the Department of Defense and others in creating this package, and it may conduct its own fact-finding activities.

Recommendations by the Department of Defense have usually been the starting point for the commission's work and likely would be so again. But how the Department of Defense creates these recommendations should be reconsidered. In recent rounds, it decentralized the process of developing recommendations, although the Secretary of Defense specified criteria for the military departments to use. These criteria focused on immediate cost-effectiveness considerations and were not informed by a vision of where the military base structure ought to be 20 years or more in the future. Yet such a vision is needed to deal with the long-term issues the military basing structure must confront—specifically, the training requirements that it must sustain, and the role that base structure plays in making the military attractive to families, who will influence the military members' decisions to stay or leave.

Legislation to create new BRAC authority should stipulate that the Secretary of Defense provide such a vision as a prelude to the commission's work. It should also create enduring authority for such a commission to submit just one package at the start of each presidential term, reflecting that president's recommendations on how much of the vision to pursue over the following four years. This approach would have the virtue of creating a long-term plan that rationalizes the Department of Defense's base structure while making immediate progress toward achieving it in a manner that gives individual communities a reasonable degree of certainty about what the intermediate future holds for them—an issue of great concern to Congress.

AMERICA'S KEY ALLIANCES

A Broader U.S.-European Strategic Partnership

Western Europe is—after the United States—the repository of the world's greatest concentration of economic capacity, military strength, and ability to undertake efforts in other important regions. So far, there has been no agreement within NATO to consider undertaking military actions outside of Europe—beyond the cooperation programs of the Partnership for Peace—but in the future, challenges to Western interests may call upon U.S.-European joint efforts elsewhere. In time, the development of the European Security and Defense Policy (ESDP) may lead the Europeans to be more outward-looking. It is also very much in the common interest that the Europeans increase their capabilities for power projection, both for NATO and for ESDP.

We recommend that, early in your administration, you begin conducting a strategic dialogue directly with the EU, in addition to the central U.S. strategic engagement with the NATO allies. This would include creating the basis for common transatlantic approaches and joint action—including continuing efforts in the Balkans, Central Europe, and Russia, and new efforts elsewhere in the world and in international institutions. This strategic dialogue will be particularly important in dealing with developments where multilateral action is both more likely to be successful than independent action and more likely to gain popular and congressional support in the United States.

Regarding potential military action, experience shows that the United States will at times need to rely upon "coalitions of the willing and able" rather than NATO as a whole. In nonmilitary areas, the United States and Western Europe should begin forging a new partnership for common action, with leadership shared between the United States and the EU, and with a major role for the private sector. Beyond Europe, this can be particularly important and effective regarding Africa—virtually an entire continent that has lost, with the end of the Cold War, a compelling rationale for Western attention. Furthermore, on issues such as migration, disease, environmental degradation, humanitarian crises, globalization, and the most basic requirements for sustaining life and promoting social, political, and economic development, the United States and the EU in combination have great potential for making a major and often decisive difference in many parts of the developing world.

You should thus consider making a new U.S.-European partnership for the 21st century a major initiative early in your administration. Like initiatives during earlier administrations—e.g., the creation of the Organization for Economic Cooperation and Development in the Kennedy administration, the National Endowment for Democracy in the Reagan administration, and the Partnership for Peace in the Clinton administration—such a U.S.-EU initiative to combine purpose and resources could meld national interests, shared values, and inspiration to deal with the challenges of this particular moment. You could launch this initiative prior to your projected summit meeting with the EU in Stockholm in June 2001.

NATO: Enlargement 2002 and Other Key Concerns. At the Washington NATO summit in April 1999, the allies agreed that they would meet at that level again, "no later than 2002," and that at that time they would review the progress made by the countries that have applied to join NATO. There are nine at the moment: six are in southeastern Europe and the Balkans (Albania, Bulgaria, Macedonia, Romania, Slovakia, and Slovenia), and three are in the Baltic region (Estonia, Latvia, and Lithuania). It is possible that one or more additional countries (Croatia and/or Austria) will apply to join NATO by 2002.

On this issue, the United States—and more particularly you, as U.S. president—will be expected to take the lead. In the end, it is the willingness of the United States to make the basic strategic commitment that is most important (certainly to the applicants), and what you decide has a strong chance of prevailing within the alliance.

We believe that you will need to decide this basic issue in 2001 and make clear the U.S. preference. In theory, you do not have to bless the principle of continued NATO enlargement, but as noted above, that would represent a major change in both U.S. and allied policy, and it would have serious negative consequences both for the alliance and for U.S. credibility across the Continent. At a more practical level, you (along with the allies) could decide to postpone the next round of enlargement past 2002. If you choose this course, however, you and the other allies would need, relatively early in 2001, to devise some unique and powerful means to convince the applicants (and other observers) that NATO had not abandoned its pledge of an "open door" to NATO enlargement.

It has already become clear that "NATO enlargement" is not an act by itself. Taking in new countries is only one element; assuring other applicants that they are not being left out (the "open door") is equally consequential, as is the Partnership for Peace, along with the NATO-Ukraine Charter and the U.S.-Baltic Charter. It is also important to continue trying to build a positive relationship with Russia, while ensuring that NATO retains a monopoly in deciding which countries to admit—e.g., denying Moscow's redlines, including those around the Baltic states. Ukraine is also a concern, and NATO has forged a special relationship with it; and the United States has negotiated a Baltic Charter with the three Baltic states. Finally, the alliance's other reforms also need to proceed: the relationship with the ESDP, internal command structure changes, and continued NATO responsibility for keeping the peace in the former Yugoslavia.

At the same time, both within your administration and in leading the alliance, it will be necessary in 2001 to craft a comprehensive strategy for enlargement—one that considers directions, pace, and practical limits (despite the "open door") and that includes continued reflection about NATO's overall goals and purposes.

These are the minimum steps—and the comprehensive package—that we believe you will need to pursue in 2001 in order to make critical NATO decisions in 2002. The actual making of choices—especially choices such as between Baltic and Balkan countries—will be intense within the alliance; this report does not suggest what these choices should be, only how to enable you to make them.

Early in your administration, several other NATO issues are likely to be important. We single out four:

- The alliance needs to continue modernizing its forces, both to enable tomorrow's allied militaries to fight together, despite rapid technological advance in the United States, and to enable the alliance to decide where, if at all, to project military power—whether in Europe or beyond. U.S. leadership is critical in keeping NATO from being "hollowed out."

- European defense industries are now consolidating, and whether they will be outward- or inward-looking will depend in major part on the willingness of the United States to lower its own barriers to industry cooperation and defense trade across the Atlantic.

- The EU continues to develop its ESDP as part of its broader Common Foreign and Security Policy. Your leadership will be important in demonstrating U.S. support for the ESDP while encouraging the Europeans to create military capabilities that will also serve NATO's needs.

- The U.S. debate on NMD could be highly divisive within the alliance. Engaging the allies in U.S. planning and decisions will be critical to preventing this issue from having a corrosive effect on broader cooperation.

The Balkans. In October 2000, the Serbian people finally ended the rule of Slobodan Milosevic. This dramatic development reduced the risk of conflict and opened up possibilities for peaceful development of areas in and around the Yugoslav Federation. Yet despite these changes, the Balkans remain the most troubled part of Europe west of the old Soviet frontier. Stabilizing the Balkans remains a key Western interest, along with helping to put this region firmly on the path of economic development and ensuring that democracy sets down firm roots. The Balkans are also important because of proximity to the Middle East and other Western political and security concerns.

In particular, transition in Belgrade has not ended the challenge to security—or the challenge to NATO and to U.S. strategic interests. Milosevic's fall effectively ended his ability to poison the well but did not settle whether Montenegro will remain part of the Yugoslav Federation or try to go its own way. The Bosnian Serbs no longer have a demagogic and self-serving champion in Belgrade, but they are far from willing to work constructively with Croats and Muslims in one country. Macedonia is still fragile. Albania is still the economic backwater of Europe. Romania and Bulgaria are lagging in their own economic transformation while they struggle to join NATO. And Albanians and Serbs in Kosovo still have irreconcilable views about the future of that province. Further, the erosion of support among the Serbian people for Milosevic does not in and of itself reflect a mass conversion to the virtues of democracy or an embrace of the values of the Western alliance. NATO, and the United States in particular, remains deeply unpopular in Serbia. In general, the basic principle behind NATO and EU efforts in Central Europe during the past decade—to determine whether former communist societies can make the reforms needed to become fully part of the West—has not yet been validated in this region.

Thus, your administration, along with the European allies, will continue to face significant challenges in the Balkans. We counsel against assuming that the stabilization forces in Bosnia and Kosovo—SFOR and KFOR—can soon depart; and U.S. leadership within NATO still calls for a significant U.S. role. The Transition 2001 panel divides, however, on the precise nature of the U.S. role: Some members argue that the United States should continue its current role, within an agreed common NATO policy; others argue that the United States should progressively turn over to the European allies responsibility for providing ground forces in the Balkans and, if need be, elsewhere in Europe.

The EU, through means including the Southeast European Stability Pact, should take the lead in regional development, but the United States must also play its part. The most difficult issue is likely to be the future of Kosovo—whether it remains a part of Serbia or becomes independent. Your administration will be expected to take the lead in diplomacy and in the search for a viable outcome; we believe that you should decide early whether the United States favors independence, autonomy, or some third alternative in order to spur the resolution of this conflict.

Recasting U.S. Alliances in Asia

The rapid pace of developments in Asia and a wide range of basic changes will pose a critical set of challenges for the United States and for U.S. leadership during your administration. The nations of Asia, beginning with our close allies, will be watching for early signs of the direction of U.S. policy. In our judgment, this cannot be a straight-line projection of current policy. Instead, you should begin immediately after the inauguration to direct a basic review of U.S. strategy throughout Asia and make appropriate revisions to current strategy for the long term.

Most immediately, as we discussed above, your new administration should be prepared for rapid changes on the Korean peninsula that could affect the U.S. military posture in South Korea and Japan. U.S. bases in Japan and South Korea will be under increasing domestic political pressure in those countries, especially if tensions on the Korean peninsula diminish. If the United States cannot sustain forward bases in Asia, its ability to stabilize the region will be cast into serious doubt, risking a reversion to a dangerous China-Japan rivalry.

Even assuming a continued U.S. presence, Asia still faces potentially serious problems that could tear at the fabric of peace and prosperity. India and especially China are rising powers that are seeking their place in the world and in the process could challenge the regional order. India and Pakistan, both now possessing nuclear weapons, also continue their decades-old confrontation, now focusing on Kashmir, and Pakistan is itself in a deep crisis of governance. Beijing continues periodically to adopt a bellicose stance toward Taiwan. Indonesia, the most populous country in Southeast Asia, is rent by ethnic and religious tensions, and the Philippines suffers from internal unrest.

The United States and its allies should agree to the pursuit of regional stability and the prevention of hegemony by any regional power as long-term objectives. We believe that your administration needs a four-part strategy to achieve these goals:

- First, the United States should reaffirm its existing Asian bilateral relationships, especially with Japan, South Korea, Thailand, the Philippines, and Australia. As part of this process, the United States should support efforts in Japan to revise the Japanese constitution, in order to allow it to expand its security horizon beyond territorial defense and to acquire appropriate capabilities for supporting coalition operations.

- Second, the United States should enhance the ties among its bilateral alliance partners and important relations in the region by information-sharing, joint exercises, and the development of joint plans to maintain regional stability.

- Third, the United States should address any situations that might tempt others to use force. Thus, the United States could state clearly that it opposes the use of force by China against Taiwan and that it opposes a declaration of independence by Taiwan. The United States should also be prepared to help resolve the various territorial disputes in the region, including that in the South China Sea; at the same time, we should emphasize our commitment to ensure freedom of navigation and adherence to an agreed code of conduct in this area.

- Fourth, the United States should promote and lead an inclusive security dialogue among as broad a range of Asian states as possible, including ASEAN. This dialogue would not only provide for a discussion of regional conflicts and promote confidence-building, it would also encourage states to enter into the U.S.-led multilateral framework sometime in the future.

Implementing such a wide-ranging and flexible strategy in Asia will, over time, require some revisions to the current U.S. military posture in the region. The focus of American attention in Asia, which has been in the northeast, will have to shift broadly southward to deal with developments in the Western Pacific security environment. The United States should continue existing security arrangements (including basing) with South Korea and Japan but also should seek to recast them. For example, in Japan, establishing forward operating locations for U.S. Air Force fighters in the southern Ryukyu Islands would be of significant value should the United States decide to support Taiwan directly in a conflict with Mainland China.

Elsewhere in Asia, the United States should seek to solidify existing access arrangements and create new ones. For example, the Philippines' location makes it an attractive potential partner. Knitting together a coherent web of security arrangements among the United States and its core partners in Asia—Japan, Australia, and South Korea—and perhaps some of its Southeast Asian allies will demand military as well as political steps. Particularly useful would be joint exercises and the creation of procedures and mechanisms for greater information-sharing—at the strategic, operational, and tactical levels—between the United States and its core regional partners.

POWERS IN FLUX

Major Powers

Russia. Although declining in relative power, Russia is the only country that retains the military capacity to destroy the United States; thus, developments there will almost certainly be among the most consequential events of the times. We recommend that your approach to Russia be informed by the following basic principles:

- The United States should lead an alliance approach to dealing with Russia. Achieving a consensus among important allies on Russia will be critical to implementing any policy. The long-term objective should be to anchor Russia in the West.

- The United States and its allies have a critical interest in seeing a continued absence of direct threat from the Russian Federation. As part of this effort, the United States and its allies should continue to seek reductions in the Russian nuclear arsenal beyond the levels of the current arms-control agreement, firm control over that arsenal, reforms within the Russian military, and an end to any Russian role in the proliferation of nuclear weapons or other WMD.

- The NATO allies should continue efforts to stabilize Central Europe while also trying to build a positive political and military relationship with the Russian Federation.

- The United States also has an interest in a Russia that is reforming and that is prepared to play a constructive, cooperative, and non-threatening role with its neighbors. However, the principal responsibility and capacity for effecting this transformation lie with Russia. At the same time, the United States, on its own and with its allies, can help by providing assistance to Russia where that can be useful and productive and will also serve Western interests. The assistance we provide should be monitored to ensure that it is not diverted for personal gain or other corrupt purposes.

In sum, the West should continue to encourage positive developments in Russia and in its relations with the outside world, but must also be prepared to secure Western interests if Russia starts to develop in a manner hostile to the West. You should continue this basic approach and monitor the effectiveness of the balance.

A decade after the collapse of the Soviet Union, both Russia's internal situation and the potential role for the United States and others have become far more complex. Internal reforms are still far from successful; the current leadership, under Vladimir Putin, has not yet demonstrated that democracy is a high priority, but it has served notice that recentralization is. It is also not clear that the Russian Federation is prepared to pursue a basically cooperative foreign policy with regard to the West or whether it will increasingly see its interests as requiring a competitive foreign policy, including efforts to divide the Western allies.

At the same time, it is increasingly clear that Russia cannot be dealt with as though it were simply a European power. As long as Russia is a coherent entity, its interests will intersect those of the West in the Transcaucasus, Central Asia, and the Far East, notably in China. It will clearly be in the U.S. interest that Russia not develop an effective strategic partnership with China that works against U.S. and Western interests. As of now, however, despite some preliminary soundings between Moscow and Beijing, such a partnership does not seem to be in the immediate offing.

Less well known are U.S. interests in Central Asia and the Transcaucasus. Clearly, the West has a concern that these countries retain their capacity to export energy and that energy transit routes traverse territories that can be considered friendly. We judge that the U.S. interest is to support the independence of each of the eight Transcaucasian and Central Asian states and to oppose any encroachment of Russian influence that could challenge that independence, while at the same time not encouraging any of these countries to act against legitimate interests of Russia. Further, it is in the U.S. and Western interest to help broker settlements of regional conflicts, such as that in Nagorno-Karabakh, and to foster resolution of conflicts in places such as Georgia and Kyrgyzstan. Beyond pursuit of these interests, along with assistance for economic and political development, military reform (including NATO's Partnership for Peace), and the nurturing of productive relations with the Western private sector, your administration should not attempt a more ambitious strategy. Stability, not change, is the basic Western interest.

With rising strife in Chechnya and elsewhere, both spontaneously and in response to Putin's centralizing policies, other internal strife, conflict, and moves toward either greater autonomy or even independence are likely within the Russian Federation. We do not believe it should be the policy of the United States to promote the dissolution of Russia—such a policy would no doubt embitter the Russian population and its leadership and would be likely to undercut other U.S. strategic objectives. At the same time, the United States should continue to press the Russian Federation to live up to international norms, including those in the Universal Declaration of Human Rights and the Helsinki Final Act, as essential elements of its full integration in the outside world.

You should put a high premium on continued efforts to help Russia control its nuclear arsenal. You should also put a high priority on gaining Russian acquiescence to stop exports that can aid in the proliferation of WMD—notably, at this moment, assistance to Iran in developing nuclear weapons and ballistic missiles. And your administration should develop and deepen a strategic dialogue with Russia across the full range of issues, in all directions from Russia's borders and also embracing areas of potential cooperation with Russia in promoting security and stability wherever interests intersect (e.g., in the former Yugoslavia). In the development of missile defenses (national and theater), you should place great emphasis on engaging Russia in efforts to gain the best balance of preserving a good relationship with it and meeting U.S. and Western national interests.

Your administration should also explore with Russia, both bilaterally and with other nations, joint projects that can advance common interests and also global interests, especially in areas such as protection of the environment. As with the NATO-Russia relationship, there should be a constant search for areas of practical cooperation, where Russia can demonstrate its willingness and ability to fit in with the global community. Russia's role in peacekeeping, both in collaboration with Western states and within international bodies, should be encouraged.

Your administration should continue to exercise leadership both in dealing directly with the Russian Federation and in promoting efforts by other Western nations and institutions to assist Russian reform. You should continue to put heavy emphasis on the development and deepening of Russian democracy, including media freedoms and respect for human rights. But for purposes both of effectiveness and of credibility, economic relations with Russia should emphasize trade, project assistance tailored to productive areas, and private-sector investments. Your administration should continue to press the Russian leadership and the private sector to adopt codes and procedures with full transparency that can raise confidence in the West about developing economic relationships.

China. Dealing with China's potential emergence as a great power will be one of the most difficult and consequential foreign policy and national security challenges facing your administration. In developing a strategy toward China, you should keep the following in mind.

First, while China's importance is increasing, its future is still uncertain. It might remain on its current path of pragmatic modernization, recognizing that good relations with the United States are necessary because of our technological leadership, huge market for Chinese exports, military power, and influence around the world. However, China could take one of several others paths: It could become increasing unstable and even fragment; it could democratize and successfully overcome the potential problems associated with transition from authoritarianism to democracy; or it could remain authoritarian but externally become more aggressive, pushing for regional primacy and threatening important American interests in Asia. Even if China stays on its current pragmatic path, relations with the United States will not be without difficulties and countervailing pressures. Beijing sees the United States as an impediment to enforcing its sovereignty over Taiwan. The Chinese government is also concerned about U.S. human rights policies that it sees as attempting to transform the regime and turn the country into a democratic state. China's role in the proliferation of WMD and missiles is another point of contention.

Second, there is no consensus in the United States on a strategy toward China. Some regard China as a hostile power that must be contained; others hope for a positive Chinese evolution and advocate a strategy purely of engagement. As long as China remains on its current path, obtaining a domestic consensus in support of either policy will be very difficult.

It would also be difficult to convince the nation to subordinate other policy goals (including trade) to adopting a policy of containing a Chinese threat that is as yet far from manifest. To be effective, containment would require the whole-hearted cooperation of regional allies and most of the other advanced industrial countries of the world. Given the uncertain Chinese future and China's essentially nonaggressive posture, U.S. allies are unlikely to be convinced that such a hardline policy toward China is necessary. In addition, whatever leverage over Chinese policies the United States attains by means of the engagement policy (with respect to such issues as sales of missiles or WMD-related technology) would be lost. Containment seems unnecessarily to resign itself to an unfavorable outcome while overlooking the possibility that Sino-U.S. relations might evolve in a much more acceptable fashion.

There is some basis for hoping that China will evolve into a cooperative and democratic state. The further opening of China to the world, including increased travel and communications and the growth of a middle class, raises the possibility of domestic transformation. Although that process could produce aggressive external behavior, the attainment of democracy might also lead China to pursue cooperative relations with other democracies. However, this outcome is far from certain. In the event that China does become hostile, a strategy purely of engagement would serve only to help China become a more threatening adversary in the future.

Given this hopeful, yet uncertain, outlook, your administration should consider, in cooperation with regional allies, pursuing a mixed strategy toward China. This strategy would engage China through commerce and through the encouragement of increased economic and political development in the hope that this process will make China more cooperative and democratic. Under this strategy, your administration would develop and deepen a strategic dialogue with China across the full range of issues and strengthen military-to-military ties. And your administration would also explore with China, both bilaterally and with other nations, joint projects that can advance common interests and also global interests, especially in areas such as protection of the environment. Of course, your administration would continue to put heavy emphasis on the development of democracy in China, including political and media freedoms and respect for human rights.

Simultaneously, the United States would hedge against any Chinese push for regional domination and seek to convince the Chinese leadership that such a push would be difficult and extremely risky to pursue. The primary manifestations of this hedge are the creation of the complex web of regional alliance relationships and agreement with our allies, including Israel and other countries such as Russia, on a list of military equipment and related technologies that should not be transferred to Beijing.

Under this mixed strategy, the United States would be agnostic on some of the key judgments about China's future—for example, whether China's enmeshing in the international system will modify its long-term objectives and behavior, and whether China as a rising power will inevitably upset Asian regional stability. A mixed strategy therefore is a flexible approach during this period of great Chinese transition. If China chooses to cooperate with the current international system and becomes increasingly democratic, this policy could evolve into mutual accommodation and partnership. If China becomes a hostile power bent on regional domination, the U.S. posture could turn into containment. The former is very much to be preferred; whether the latter can be avoided is primarily up to China.

Regional Powers

India and Pakistan. Your administration will also confront important challenges and opportunities in South Asia. The continuing violence in Kashmir and the risk of a larger war between India and Pakistan—that might include the use of nuclear weapons now in the possession of both countries—have made this region (in President Clinton's words) "the most dangerous place on earth."

Both India and Pakistan are currently in the midst of major domestic transformations. The Indian economy has been growing at a rate of roughly 7 percent since 1991, and most international observers believe that growth can continue; this would make India the world's fourth largest economy (in purchasing-power-parity terms) by 2015. An economy of that size would increase India's ability to modernize its military forces, develop a credible nuclear deterrent, and deepen U.S.-Indian economic linkages. In short, if current trends hold, India will emerge as a great power.

India's democratic institutions remain both durable and robust. However, the traditionally liberal and secular character of the state is increasingly contested by a variety of new Hindu fundamentalist groups in Indian politics.

The situation in Pakistan remains unsettled and troublesome on multiple counts. Pakistan continues to be beset by unhealthy political, economic, and strategic trends that have become both intractable and mutually reinforcing. The most disturbing of these trends has been the growth of Islamic extremism. Extremist groups thrive because of Pakistan's continuing state failures and because they are intentionally supported by the Pakistani military and secret services in the pursuit of the latter's goals in Kashmir and Afghanistan.

Politically, the disruption of democratic governance resulting from the military coup in October 1999 is likely to continue well into the foreseeable future, and the military is likely to be formally involved in governance even after General Pervez Musharraf leaves office. The Pakistani economy remains paralyzed by high external indebtedness and low levels of education in the workforce. Finally, Pakistan's strategic circumstances also remain highly unsettled. Pakistan refuses to roll back its nuclear program and continues to rely on assistance from China and North Korea for future strategic technologies because of its continuing fears about India's capabilities and intentions. Pakistan appears committed to using its emerging nuclear capabilities for strategic cover as it challenges India through its support for insurgents in Kashmir. Islamabad also sponsors the Taliban in Afghanistan. Given the Taliban's ties with terrorists such as Osama bin Laden, the threat they pose to stability in Central Asia, and the possibility that Taliban-style Islamic extremism might spread even to Pakistan itself, Pakistani policies have the potential to pose a broader challenge to U.S. interests.

We recommend that your South Asian policy proceed from a decoupling of India and Pakistan in U.S. calculations. That is, U.S. relations with each state must be governed by an objective assessment of the intrinsic value of each country to American interests in this new era. This means recognizing that India is on its way to becoming a major Asian power and therefore warrants both a level of engagement far greater than the previous norm and an appreciation of its potential for both collaboration and resistance across a much larger canvas than simply South Asia. In the case of Pakistan, it means recognizing that this is a country in serious crisis and that it is pursuing policies that run counter to important U.S. interests. You should avoid isolating Pakistan and be prepared to assist in dampening the currently disturbing social and economic trends by reaching out to Pakistani society. But you should also consider increased pressure—including using the leverage of international financial assistance—to curb Islamabad's sponsorship of extremist groups such as the Taliban and to gain Pakistan's cooperation in the fight against international terrorism. These observations imply the following policies for your administration.

With India:

1. Continue high-level bilateral political consultations on key political and strategic issues, with the aim of developing common approaches to the key emerging challenges of global order: terrorism, stability in Asia, WMD proliferation, peace operations, and others.

2. Encourage Indian integration into multilateral security and economic organizations in the Asia-Pacific region.

3. Strengthen economic cooperation at all levels—including efforts to remove the remaining economic sanctions—with an emphasis on removing bureaucratic impediments to trade in civilian high technology and increasing bilateral economic flows.

4. Work to enhance military-to-military cooperation in the form of joint exchanges, training, exercises, and eventually joint operations, wherever possible.

With Pakistan:

1. Encourage economic reform.

2. Extend assistance in strengthening the institutions in civil society, with the objective of helping Pakistan become a modern Muslim republic. In particular, this would involve support for Pakistani NGOs working in education, health care, and women's rights.

3. Maintain pressure on the current regime for a return to democracy.

4. Increase pressure on the regime to stop providing support for the Taliban and to cooperate in the fight against terrorism.

5. Clearly communicate to Pakistan's civilian and military leadership your strong preference for restraint in Kashmir.

6. Work to restore some forms of military-to-military cooperation short of arms sales, primarily in the form of personnel exchanges and military education.

Iraq and Iran. For the past several years, the United States has pursued a so-called dual containment policy in the Persian Gulf. However, changing circumstances—including erosion of sanctions against Iraq, political change in Iran, and a new regional dynamic that also includes Pakistan and Afghanistan—call for a major review of this policy and possible changes to it. We recommend that at the outset of your administration, whether or not the United States is immediately challenged by Saddam Hussein, you direct a basic review and analysis of overall U.S. interests and policy in the Persian Gulf region. This review would start from the premise that a critical long-term goal is to maintain regional stability and prevent the domination of the Persian Gulf by a hostile power and would cover several issues, including the following:

- *Whether regime change in Iraq is necessary to U.S. long-term goals and, if so, how to bring it about.* The United States needs either to reduce its objectives in Iraq, which at present include regime overthrow, or to change its strategy so that it might hope to achieve these objectives. If you decide to increase the U.S. emphasis on regime change, you must first ensure that strong support exists, in both the public and the Congress, for the use of force against the Iraqi regime and build on that support with substantial efforts to strengthen the anti-Saddam opposition. Measures could involve increasing the military training and funding offered to opposition figures, greatly increasing the funding of the opposition, attempts to divide the regime and the military, extending the no-fly zone to the entire country, and conducting air strikes on military targets in conjunction with opposition military operations. Gaining the support of allies and other regional states for such a policy, however, would not be easy.

- *Whether, by contrast, our goal should be limited to containing Iraq.* This goal would have four key parts: ensuring deterrence of direct Iraqi aggression against any of its neighbors and, if need be, sufficient force to defeat any such aggression; continuing efforts to constrain Iraqi programs to develop WMD (as discussed above) with key emphasis on building support among allies and regional states for whatever measures are needed to achieve this goal; continuing to reduce opportunities for Iraqi propaganda within the region; and supporting states, especially Jordan, that are vulnerable to Iraqi economic and other pressures. The threat from Iraq, especially its missiles and WMD programs, is likely to grow in this case.

- *Iran's role in the Persian Gulf, including whether it could, in time, play a robust role in containing Iraq, consistent with Western interests.* This would require Iran's ceasing to be a source of challenge, threat, and instability—currently measured in terms of support for terrorism, active opposition to Arab-Israeli peace negotiations, and efforts to develop WMD. Whether that will be possible within the next few years is not clear.

- *What long-term U.S. military posture in the region, including the Fifth Fleet and onshore deployments, is needed to promote our interests and those of regional and allied states.* This should include analysis of whether it could prove possible to create greater regional and allied responsibility for security, beyond basic containment of Iraq. In time, this should be an objective of U.S. policy, so that the United States will not have to assume the major share of the burden of dealing with regional problems.

- *How U.S. allies, especially in Europe, might contribute to the containment of Iraq.* The more broadly containment of Iraq is based, the more effective it will be. The new strategic dialogue with the EU, recommended above, might be an effective forum for drawing Europe into a more effective partnership in the Persian Gulf.

In addition to security issues in the Persian Gulf that derive in significant part from the role played by Iraq and, in particular, Saddam

Hussein, the United States has broader interests in the future of Iran. President Mohammed Khatami's election in May 1997 reflected the desire of most Iranians for political reform, greater freedom, and reform of the flagging Iranian economy. Khatami's efforts at international reintegration have already improved ties with Europe and the Middle East and have allowed greater political freedom within Iran. However, Khatami's agenda is not embraced by hardliners, including the Supreme Leader, Ayatollah Ali Khamenei; the leadership of the important religious foundations; and unknown numbers of people in the military, the intelligence community, and the security services. These hardliners have thwarted Khatami's domestic agenda.

Another factor could allow improved U.S.-Iranian relations. That is the emergence of Pakistan and a Taliban-controlled Afghanistan at the top of Iran's foreign policy agenda. Iranian policymakers are deeply concerned about threats from and by Pakistan and Afghanistan. These threats include a serious refugee problem, drugs and weapons smuggling, and a rivalry for influence in Central Asia. The pragmatists dominating the Iranian foreign ministry believe that Tehran and Washington share a common interest in Afghanistan and Pakistan. However, U.S. policymakers should understand that because Iran's drive to acquire nuclear weapons is motivated by its concerns about a nuclear Pakistan, as well as by Saddam Hussein's continuing attempt to develop a nuclear capability, even an Iran that is dominated by pragmatists is unlikely to abandon its WMD and missile programs until it feels more secure in the region.

The United States cannot determine the outcome of the power struggle in Iran. It would be foolhardy to champion President Khatami and thus to undermine him further in the eyes of those who oppose him and who would use support by the United States as a means to question his commitment to the Islamic Republic. Suspicion about and unhappiness with the United States run deep in Iran. Nonetheless, we recommend that your administration be prepared both to continue a containment policy, if that is necessary, and to seize the opportunity if the Iranian pragmatists become more dominant and Iran becomes more interested in rapprochement with the United States. Approaching the United States will not be easy for the pragmatists in Iran and will require them to show results quickly. In particular, your administration should consider being ready with specific ideas on:

- Increasing U.S. investments in Iranian infrastructure, particularly in the energy sector.

- Ending U.S. opposition to building an energy pipeline through Iran from Central Asia.

- Achieving cooperation between the United States and Iran on containing Iraq and on stabilizing Afghanistan and Pakistan, with the ultimate goal of stopping Iran's WMD programs.

Indonesia. Indonesia is undergoing a political transformation that could change the geostrategic shape of Asia. Its huge population—the fourth largest in the world—and its strategic location, straddling key sea-lanes, make its stability and future path a critical U.S. interest. The best-case scenario would be Indonesia's evolution toward a more stable and democratic state. Unfortunately, that evolution is threatened by a weak governing coalition, numerous insurgencies and separatist movements, and the looming presence of a military that views itself as the ultimate guardian and arbiter of the Indonesian state.

The current period will be critical in defining Indonesia's future. The country today faces the most serious threat to its stability and territorial integrity since its independence more than 50 years ago. The separation of East Timor encouraged secessionist movements in even more economically and politically important provinces. There has also been widespread ethnic and religious violence in eastern Indonesia. Indonesians themselves fear that the violence could lead to a wider sectarian conflict that could tear Indonesia apart or spur a reversion to military authoritarianism.

Severe instability in, or a breakup of, Indonesia has the potential to disrupt trade and investment flows throughout Asia; to generate widespread violence; to create massive refugee flows; to encourage secessionist movements throughout Southeast Asia; and to damage the progress of democracy in the region. Therefore, doing what we can to help avoid political collapse in Indonesia and to keep democratic reforms on track should be a high priority for the U.S. government.

The United States has a limited capacity to influence internal events in Indonesia. Nonetheless, an active policy of engagement that supports the maintenance of Indonesia's territorial integrity and the survival of its democratic experiment can only help its transition. This policy might include the following elements:

- *Understanding the limits of what the Indonesian government can deliver.* The democratic transformation of Indonesia has only begun and will take time. Pushing Indonesia too far or too fast on sensitive issues such as civil-military relations would risk undermining the current democratic government's standing with key domestic constituencies.

- *Supporting Indonesia's economic recovery and territorial integrity.* Economic recovery is the key to political stability and democratic development, but achieving it will require strong support from the international community. The United States, in cooperation with its Asian partners, particularly Japan, Singapore, and Australia, should provide the necessary technical and financial assistance.

- *Engaging the Indonesian military.* For better or for worse, the Indonesian military will play a critical role in the process of Indonesia's transformation. The United States has an opportunity to influence the military's thinking at a time when it is looking for a new model and open to new ideas.

- *Helping to restore a constructive Indonesian role in regional security.* Before the 1997–98 crisis, Indonesia served as a keystone of stability in Southeast Asia. Restoring this role will require working with the UN to stabilize the situation on Timor and working with Australia to rehabilitate the Indonesian-Australian security relationship.

THE NEW GLOBAL AGENDA

The end of the Cold War and radical changes in the global economy during recent years present you with a new and expanding agenda of foreign policy developments that can have important effects on the interests of the United States, its allies, and its partners. By the same token, these developments open up opportunities for the United States and others to help shape the kind of world in which we would like to live in decades to come—a world in which political, economic, social, and personal benefits are open to more people on earth than ever before.

The process of globalization—defined here as the increasing volume and speed of cross-border flows of goods, services, ideas, capital, technology, and people—means that the United States will be increasingly affected by a variety of forces that were once viewed as being limited to individual nations. Globalization will no doubt have a growing impact on the issues you will face in "foreign policy," on the instruments available, on the relative degree of control over events exercised by governments as opposed to the private sector and NGOs, and on interconnections between events in different parts of the world.

This emerging phenomenon will put a high premium in your administration on process: identifying what is happening and its significance, at home and abroad; understanding interconnections; illuminating choices and alternatives for policy; and engaging in a higher degree of strategic analysis and planning than has perhaps ever been true before. Insight, inclusiveness, strategy, and flexibility will be the key requirements for success. Here we highlight four areas: fostering global economic order and prosperity; dealing with new, nontraditional challenges and opportunities; countering asymmetric warfare; and building international institutions.

Fostering Global Economic Order and Prosperity

The United States has enormous economic strength that gives it confidence and influence around the world. Of course, in this area, your first duty as president is to promote economic growth and prosperity at home. However, developments and difficulties abroad have an increasing impact on the U.S. economy. In recent years, important U.S. interests—market-oriented reform in Russia and parts of Central Europe and the Former Soviet Union, prosperity and democracy in Mexico, stability in Asia, political and economic development in Africa—have been deeply affected by economic and financial crises. Protecting these and other interests implies several steps, including:

- *Dealing with the domestic and international effects of globalization.* Some social groups and even entire countries have been largely excluded from the prosperity and promise of globalization. This has domestic implications in the United States, especially for those industries and workers most deeply affected by globalization, and these call for domestic redress. Abroad, U.S. leadership is required to develop a modern global trading and financial system that is widely viewed as fair and equitable. The United States and its key economic partners must be willing to provide developing countries access to their home markets in exchange for sensible economic policies that can attract international capital, while devising mechanisms to reduce their exposure to the destabilizing effects of international financial crises.

- *Reinvigorating trade negotiations.* The process of trade liberalization has been at a virtual standstill—advances have been rare, while intergovernmental disputes, punitive sanctions, and street protests have dominated the headlines. As in the past, U.S. leadership will be critical. We recommend that early in your administration, you seek "fast-track" trade negotiating authority from Congress; secure support from key allies on management of the large and complex multilateral negotiations; engage U.S. groups with critical interests—now notably including labor and environmental practices in some U.S. trading partners; and work to ensure that less-influential countries and NGOs gain appropriate access to the process of negotiation.

- *Reforming global financial markets.* The international financial crises of the late 1990s have shown the limitations of global financial markets for self-regulation and self-adjustment. Your administration has the opportunity and the leverage to play a critical role in reform during the next several years. Your leadership can encourage cooperative steps that can make crises less frequent and less severe. Guidelines include:

  — *Financial transparency is essential.* The United States and its allies should use their financial leverage to create minimum international standards of accountability that are recognized and adhered to throughout the world.

  — *Openness to international capital flows requires a strong domestic financial system that can absorb sudden reverses in capital flows and allocate capital inflows to productive uses.*

Developing countries will require international assistance in creating such a financial system.

— *Heavy reliance by either the public or private sector on short-term international credit promotes instability.* The United States should not interfere with sensible efforts by developing countries to limit short-term speculative capital flows.

• *Reforming the international financial institutions.* International financial institutions such as the International Monetary Fund (IMF), the World Bank, and the multilateral investment banks have, in general, developed credibility problems, which have weakened their capacity to fulfill their mandated functions of providing emergency financing during crises and serving as reliable sources of finance for development. We suggest that, early in your administration, you work with key economic partners to promote reforms in their operations to ensure that they are accountable to their constituencies in both lending and borrowing countries; that fund flows are stimulating balanced and sustainable growth; and that these funds are neither being diverted or stolen by host-country officials nor allocated to inefficient or socially irresponsible uses. Your administration should also consider acting to ensure that international financial institutions do not serve as guarantors of unwise investments made by private institutions and individuals.

• *Extending and deepening economic ties with Latin America.* The United States has a strategic and economic interest in a stable, democratic, and free-market-oriented Latin America. In the 1990s, Latin America and the Caribbean became the United States' fastest-growing regional market and a potential partner in what could some day be the largest free trade area in the world. In particular, Mexico is undergoing a historic political transition. This transition means that the United States will have an opportunity to work with President-elect Vicente Fox's administration to deepen the U.S.-Mexican relationship and Mexico's integration into the North American market. At the same time, the disruptive impact of globalization, a lack of economic development in many countries, and the activities of the transnational criminal cartels have given rise to a variety of new threats to democracy and stability in Latin America, particularly in the Andean region. Meeting these new challenges will require more than traditional diplomatic and military responses. It will also require a proactive U.S. economic policy toward Latin America, informed by the requirements of building an institutional framework for open markets and a stable democratic order in the hemisphere. The key components of this policy would include efforts to promote economic development, ensure monetary stability, extend and deepen free trade areas throughout Latin America, and foster the development of a hemispheric security community.

Nontraditional Threats and Opportunities

A number of developments, especially emanating from what used to be combined as the "developing world," can, over time, pose severe challenges to Western society. These include uncontrolled migration across borders and regions; international crime; disease, especially pandemics like AIDS; and the broad range of issues and concerns that shelter under the overarching term "environment."

In few of these or similar areas is there a U.S. national consensus that these issues represent serious "security" threats to the United States or allied and partner societies. This report does not suggest judgments you should make about the key items on this list; rather, it proposes that what your administration does may have a major effect on whether these problems become more or less daunting.

In some cases it will be difficult to understand any linkages—e.g., if the developed world does not reengage in sub-Saharan Africa, will its problems be visited directly either on the nationals of the major powers or on their own territories? But the case is clear that, in this era, the United States has the resources and opportunity to ask itself whether it wants to live in a world where such problems continue to fester or whether it will try to make a difference. For your administration, this is first and foremost a matter of leadership and exhortation; then it is a matter of developing productive alliances with like-minded, relatively wealthy countries to begin creating a new ethos about the future that is not based solely on a short-term national model, but which sees a long-term, collective moral dimension.

Clearly, your administration should continue the U.S. government's vigorous commitment to human rights and democracy. This is the major opportunity of the age, in terms of creating the basis for a world in which more people than ever before will be able to be secure in their persons, take part in civil society, and pursue benefits for themselves and their families. Unstinting U.S. support for human rights need no longer be limited, in terms of country or region, by the ambiguities and tradeoffs that were sometimes required during the Cold War. Democracy is perhaps the most formidable social and political force in the world, both today and for the indefinite future. The United States—and your administration—must remain the foremost champion of democratic development, in word and deed, including vigorous support for global democracy-based institutions, follow-up to the June 2000 World Democracy Conference in Warsaw, and democracy-oriented NGOs.

Asymmetric Warfare

During your administration, key challenges to U.S. power—and to the security of the United States, its allies, and its friends—can come from so-called asymmetric warfare: the capacity of smaller powers (or nonstate actors) to cause damage to U.S. interests through the use of unusual techniques, out of proportion to their inherent power and position. Moreover, the transnational nature of these challenges means that the U.S. ability to effectively counter threats from asymmetric warfare will depend to a great extent on the partnerships forged with allies and like-minded states. We judge the following three areas to be most important:

Terrorism. In response to U.S. military dominance, a number of countries—and nonstate actors—have been developing means of trying to offset or even neutralize U.S. advantages. With the exception of WMD (especially nuclear weapons), few will pose serious strategic threats to the United States or its allies, although tactical military developments can have significant impact on the battlefield. But terrorism, including terrorism within the United States, remains a threat, not just to the capacity of Americans to work and travel in some parts of the world, but also to a sense of personal security. You will need to place high priority on continuing efforts to neutralize terrorists, using both established and new techniques. This includes technical responses, vigorous pursuit of terrorists, and—where possible—efforts to reduce or eliminate the political motivations (or sources of political tolerance) for terrorism. Your administration should also be alert to the possibility that terrorism could be brought to our shores and should continue funding programs to counter it.

Cyber threats. In terms of potential disruption or damage to the United States and other Western states, threats to cyber networks must rank among the critical challenges to U.S. strategic interests—in this case, including economic interests—that could develop during your presidency. The sources, type, scope, and effectiveness of such cyber threats are poorly understood. Areas of uncertainty include the degree to which the U.S. economy and society have vulnerabilities that can be identified and protected, as well as the degree to which redundancies enable global networks to be largely "self-healing." Nevertheless, this is an area in which robust U.S. activity to identify potential threats and to take actions to counter them is essential. Your administration's leadership will be critical.

WMD and missiles. Weapons of mass destruction and the means of delivering them will proliferate, for a variety of reasons. Ambitions and insecurities will lead states and subnational groups, including terrorists, to seek these weapons. Knowledge, technologies, and materials are becoming more widely available. Controlling exports of sensitive technologies has become more difficult as their commercial uses have expanded. Governments find themselves under increasing political and economic pressures to relax export controls. Russia, China, and North Korea continue to sell equipment and technologies. Moreover, states are increasingly able to produce many components indigenously, thereby decreasing the effectiveness of traditional nonproliferation instruments such as export controls, economic sanctions, and military interdiction.

Even beyond these difficulties, U.S. nonproliferation policies lack integration with allies and partners and indeed diverge markedly from those of other states. Some other governments tend to view the proliferation threat as less serious and more amenable to amelioration through political engagement with both the proliferators and those who supply the equipment and technologies. Indeed, few governments are willing to risk political relations or economic trade to promote nonproliferation goals.

Your administration's leadership can have an important effect on both slowing the rate and reducing the consequences of proliferation. The chief lesson of the past, however, is that unilateral approaches are rarely effective. Export controls mean little if alternative suppliers are willing to sell. Sanctions have little bite if honored by only a few. A successful nonproliferation strategy will require U.S. leadership in promoting greater cooperation among the major industrial countries, some of which will need to change their assessment of the threat's seriousness, their confidence in strategies of political engagement, and their willingness to undertake difficult political and economic steps.

Further, we recommend that you mandate cooperation among our law-enforcement, intelligence, economic, and diplomatic assets to combat WMD and missile proliferation. Internationally, the United States should press for strengthening the Biological Weapons Convention, press Russia to stop providing any assistance for nuclear programs, and discourage Chinese and Russian assistance in the spread of missile technology.

Developing International Institutions

Finally, the United States naturally wants to maintain its current position of being relatively free from external threats and relatively capable of shaping the global environment. One long-term means is particularly critical: U.S. leadership in building international institutions, practices, attitudes, and processes that can benefit the United States precisely because they also benefit other countries. The value of this approach was demonstrated by the recreation of NATO during the Bush and Clinton administrations, to the extent that now, potentially, a wide range of countries spanning the Continent can find in the reformed alliance something positive to benefit both their own security and the development of their societies. The EU has also made great strides, not only for its 15 member states, but also for many countries in Central Europe and beyond.

No doubt, neither the NATO nor the EU model will find direct application elsewhere; both are the products of unusual circumstances. But as U.S. president, you have the opportunity to foster the basic method of institutional development. This is a method that can help gain broad support for action in those parts of the world—e.g., major parts of Africa and Asia—where classic models of geopolitics or immediate self-interest are inadequate for addressing serious problems. In our view, sustaining support for this approach will require rebuilding the effectiveness of the UN as an institution and reestablishing U.S. domestic support for the UN. This will require paying the dues that the United States owes to the UN, while pressing for needed institutional reforms.

COMMENTS AND DISSENT BY TRANSITION 2001 PANEL MEMBERS

It is my view and concern that the single most important issue regarding the future of the nation's security rests in attracting and retaining sufficient numbers of qualified people to serve in government. This deficiency extends throughout government and to all levels of seniority, particularly career public servants. Therefore, restoring government service as a respected, important and rewarding calling must be one of the administration's highest priorities. Captain John Paul Jones put this in perspective more than two centuries ago, observing that "men [and by extension women] are more important than guns in the rating of a ship." That sentiment applies even more strongly today. No matter the urgency of competing and timely national security challenges, uncertainties and dangers, people are what make any organization succeed or fail.

— Harlan Ullman

While I agree with most of the report, there are several points on which I differ or dissent, and a couple of points that I feel should be added.

I am not yet persuaded that a national missile defense will increase our national security, either in its own right—given the likely impact on relations with allies and adversaries—or in relation to other uses of the funds—parts of the 050 or 150 [see, for example, the report's argument regarding procurement, pay and maintenance] accounts which promise more credible contributions to security and threat reduction. With that in mind, I disagree with the report's predisposition to embrace NMD and to debate only the alternative technologies. This also bears on the report's support for significant increases in defense modernization and compensation, which presumes continuation of current strategy. While the report urges an early and comprehensive review of that strategy, its DOD spending recommendation appears to prejudge the results of that review.

The recommendation of increased support for Colombia and neighboring states is valid as far as it goes. Given that the Colombian crisis is largely rooted in the problem of U. S. demand for narcotics, the report should not stop short of recommending a major effort to deal with demand reduction at home. While perhaps nominally a "domestic" issue, U.S. illicit drug consumption clearly has direct consequences for international security.

The report merely references nontraditional threats. While it may be accurate to say that there is no consensus about the seriousness of these threats, I want to enter a strong individual plea that the next administration treat them—especially disease, population and the environment—as deserving high-level attention.

Not surprisingly, as a set of recommendations to the next President, the report has an executive branch bias. There is the requisite counsel to consult with, and develop the support of, Congress. We should caution, however, that the long-term efficacy of executive power in the foreign relations and national security areas depends on its being grounded in an understanding on the part of the American people and their representatives in Congress of our role in the world, of the need for our leadership, and of the limits of our power. Only the President is in a position to conduct this necessary, on-going instruction in world affairs and U.S. responsibilities.

In a similar vein, beyond dealing with the usual components of foreign and national security policy, the comprehensive review of strategy we urge in the report should also extend to an examination of the style and manner in which U.S. influence and power is exercised. It may well be that our national self-interest will be better served by an approach to other nations which is more respectful and collaborative, which might be characterized by a certain humility of power.

— David Skaggs

In Chapter Two, this report sets out all the right questions that must be answered before a decision can be made on whether to develop and deploy a national missile defense. These include effects on U.S. relations with China, Russia and Europe, assessment of alternative means of threat reduction, cost relative to other needs and the technological feasibility of an adequately effective system. The report presupposes the answers, however, by stipulating that the U.S. must have an NMD. Since in my judgment no system has yet been described that appears technologically realistic within a reasonable time frame and whose geostrategic benefits decisively outweigh its costs, I can not subscribe to this conclusion.

In its discussion of Regional Powers (Chapter Three), the report outlines a U.S. policy towards India which fails to mention the single issue that now most bedevils and will continue to frame the relationship. That issue, of course, is what the U.S. attitude should be towards India's new overt nuclear weapons status and its ongoing— albeit slow motion—progress on weaponization. Should the U.S. attempt to rollback India's nuclear status? Sanction it? Accept it? Try to influence its pace and scale? Try to reduce its dangers through assistance on intelligence, doctrine, safety, and command and control? How, in short, can the U.S. best reconcile the reality of India's place in the world with the U.S.'s global responsibility to curb nuclear proliferation? No discussion that sidesteps this issue can provide helpful advice on this important relationship.

Also in this section, the treatment of Iraq argues that a policy that drops regime change as an essential U.S. goal would *increase* the threat from Iraq's missile and WMD programs. ("The threat from Iraq, especially its missiles and WMD programs, is likely to grow in this case.") The likely outcome, I believe, is exactly the opposite. Replacing our current policy of advocating the removal of Saddam Hussein from power, a policy not supported by our allies, for a policy that focused on "building support among allies and regional states for whatever measures are needed" to constrain Iraqi WMD programs, would be far more likely to command others' support and therefore far more likely to succeed in *reducing* the WMD threat. This is a crucial policy choice before the next administration.

Finally, I must point out that a report that advocates a policy of "selective global leadership" but fails to mention U.S. policy toward the United Nations and other major global institutions (neither NATO nor the EU is relevant here), has missed the point. *Selective* global leadership appropriately implies burden sharing. Yes, our alliances should be revitalized, but there are a growing number of global problems from failed states to terrorism to climate change, that require global governance. There are global norms that must be built and strengthened that will carry part of the load. There are problems that can *only* be dealt with in broader fora. There is the rule of law we count on others to obey that is undermined, for example, by our failure to honor a legal commitment to pay our UN dues. In short, policies necessary to establish U.S. credibility to successfully exercise "selective global leadership" are missing here. Military strength is necessary but not sufficient.

Jessica T. Mathews

These comments do not necessarily reflect the opinions of the Transition 2001 panel.